GOSPEL SPIRITUALITY AND CATHOLIC WORSHIP

Integrating Your Personal Prayer Life and Liturgical Experience

Paul L. Cioffi, S.J.
William P. Sampson, S.J.

PAULIST PRESS
New York/Mahwah, N.J.

Acknowledgments

Grateful acknowledgment is made for permission to use the following: Excerpts reprinted from *Service Book and Hymnal,* copyright © 1958 by permission of Augsburg Fortress, Minneapolis, Minnesota. Excerpts from the English translation of *Rite of Holy Week* © 1972, International Committee on English in the Liturgy, Inc. (ICEL); excerpts from the English translation of *The Roman Missal* © 1973, ICEL. All rights reserved. Scripture excerpts marked (NAB) are taken from the New American Bible © 1970 Confraternity of Christian Doctrine, Inc., Washington, D.C. Used with permission. All rights reserved. No part of the New American Bible may be reproduced by any means without permission in writing from the copyright owner.

Cover design by Morris Berman Studio

Library of Congress Cataloging-in-Publication Data

Cioffi, Paul L., 1928-
    Gospel spirituality and Catholic worship : integrating your personal prayer life and liturgical experience / Paul L. Cioffi, William P. Sampson.
        p. cm.
    Includes bibliographical references.
    ISBN 0-8091-4010-1
    1. Lord's Supper—Catholic Church. 2. Spirituality—Catholic Church. 3. Lord's Supper—Celebration. 4. Catholic Church—Doctrines. I. Sampson, William P. II. Title.

BX2215.2 .C5 2000
264'.02—dc21

                                                                        00-063696

Published by Paulist Press
997 Macarthur Boulevard
Mahwah, New Jersey 07430

www.paulistpress.com

Printed and bound in the United States of America

Contents

The authors wish to express their gratitude to
Peggy and Bill Cloherty, who initiated the process of publishing this
book, and to Brenda Carr, Borys Dackiw, Jim Alphen, and especially
to the late Tom Dorris who helped with the editing.

We also wish to thank
the Carr, Odierna and Wentzel families who gave us
the space and isolation to do much of our writing.

"My brothers and sisters,
to prepare ourselves
to celebrate the sacred mysteries,
let us call to mind our sins."

(*Sacramentary,* Penitential Rite: Introduction C)

Preface

E normous energy has been expended in trying to make the Eucharist more meaningful ever since the Second Vatican Council enacted *The Constitution on the Liturgy* in December 1963. Laypeople as well as clergy got involved in implementing the reforms decreed by the Council and the Congregation for Divine Worship. Organists, music directors, and songwriters took up the task of getting the congregation to join in the singing. Scholars and popular writers tried to explain the changes that were taking place. Sermons became opportunities to explain the importance of active participation in the liturgy by the whole congregation.

The purpose of this book is to help priests and all Catholics to enter into the Eucharist at its deepest level, to experience it in its fullness, so that they can pray the eucharistic prayers as their own personal prayers. Although this book is not a history of the liturgy, we look at moments in the past when liturgy and spirituality went separate ways. Both areas concern our relationship with God, but they tend to evolve along parallel lines.

We discuss the illusion-producing dynamic called *repression* that operates in human nature, leading it away from reality. We look at our tendency to avoid self-knowledge and explore how crippling this instinct is. When repression is successful, it results in spirituality and liturgy that ignore self-knowledge, the very thing the liturgy demands in order to be effective.

We then go back to the beginnings of Christian spirituality and liturgy. There, within the consciousness of Jesus, we discover the unity he saw in the two. We show how his spiritual direction of the apostles prepared them to experience the Eucharist in its fullness. What impelled Jesus to invent a rite? We show how he felt the Father leading him both in this precise form of ritual and to this way of spiritual direction.

What this study reveals is that Jesus saw himself at the center of this rite, between his "Abba" and humankind. He saw himself as our future, sharing with us his intimacy with the Father. He knew himself as the "beloved" of his Father. He felt himself as brother to every one of us. His inheritance is ours; his relationship to the Father is ours. We can glimpse the binary essence of the Godhead, a twoness of mutual loving, only when we are within Jesus. His Eucharist has this double focus, inviting us into the innermost world of the Godhead.

We show how the eucharistic rite already preaches the core gospel. Just as the early disciples, by doing what Jesus said to do, performed a rite that implied a binatarian center (without their awareness of this), we too are invited to do what we cannot comprehend. The effort to return to gospel sources of spirituality and liturgy will reveal the essential relationship between them that Jesus had in mind.

We then detail how the texts of the *Sacramentary* and the *Lectionary* richly highlight this fundamental relationship, how the texts stress now one element, now another. The mind and heart of Jesus can become the central focus of the preaching done within the Eucharist.

In the first chapter we describe the present separation of liturgy and spirituality. We briefly review the story of the modern liturgical reform and the renewal of spirituality. What brought about their separate lives? That is the problem we face today.

Chapter One

Liturgy and Spirituality

Today there is a wide audience for magazines and journals dealing with liturgy. One of the most popular is *Worship*. The focus of liturgists is exemplified by articles such as "The Eucharist as Sacrifice," "Form and Function in the Early Synagogue and Church," "The Role of Music as Ritual Symbol in Roman Catholic Liturgy," "Performance, Practice, and Meaning in Christian Baptism," "Gender Analysis and Christian Initiation," and "Liturgical Reform and the Ambrosian and Mozarabic Rites." Mention of private prayer is rare.

This is the world of liturgy today. It is a big establishment. In universities there are departments of liturgy whose professors produce books on the history of the liturgy and its theology. Parishes have full-time directors of liturgy and many people involved in this ministry.

There is also a wide audience today for magazines and journals dealing with spirituality, one of the most popular of which is *Review for Religious*. Some typical articles are "Feeling and Pain and Prayer," "The Desert and the Cell," and "Where Is God in Suffering?" Liturgy is mentioned only rarely.

Spirituality institutes offer courses on topics such as "Making Good Decisions," "Sexuality and Spirituality," "Prayer and Spiritual Direction," "Working with Our Dreams," and "Evil as a Psychological-Spiritual Necessity."

Like the world of liturgy, the world of spirituality is also a big establishment. In the universities students take courses in the history and theology of spirituality covering the desert fathers, individual mystics as well as the schools of mysticism, and the varied spiritualities of world religion today. Retreat houses provide spiritual direction for tens of thousands of people each year: retreats, weekends or days of prayer, and workshops. Full-time spiritual directors, many of them laypeople, abound.

The two worlds use two different vocabularies. Spirituality speaks of the Dark Night, discernment, mental prayer, the Love Command, methods of prayer, feelings, and repression, locating where one is in terms of emotions, consolation, and desolation. It's all about the spiritual life and the problems of private prayer. Liturgists, on the other hand, talk about active participation, sacrifice, initiation, priesthood, sacrament, rubrics, the liturgical year, the vernacular, and inculturation.

Thus today two vast influential worlds exist with large followings, resources, scholars, and popularizers. They travel along parallel paths, with different vocabularies. They don't interact except peripherally.

Yet the two are essentially related. Both try to answer the same questions: how to respond to God's initiative; how the gospel sheds light on human existence; how to grow in holiness; how to have an enlarged experience of God. How is it then that each camp almost totally ignores the other?

This is especially odd since both fields have experienced major renewals. During the first forty years of the twentieth century, because of the revival of biblical and patristic studies, there was a growing interest in the doctrine of the church as the Mystical Body of Christ, which contrasted sharply with the post-Tridentine way of viewing the church in more rational and juridical terms.

The new ecclesiology, which affirmed an organic and mysterious but real unity between Head and members and among the members themselves, rested solidly on scripture and the church fathers. However, this new concept of the church highlighted problems in parish congregations. The faithful were passive inside and outside the liturgy—they were imbued with individualistic piety and devotions. They brought this piety and these devotions to Mass, but the liturgical rites did not command their attention or invite their collaboration. There was a vast chasm between the sanctuary and the nave.

The recovery of the doctrine of the church as the Body of Christ set the stage for a renewal of the liturgy and of liturgical practice. As the church expressed the new ecclesiology in official documents, it was apparent to some liturgists that this dynamic vision of the church was not reflected in the liturgy: congregations were not joyfully involved in the corporate piety of a redeemed people at worship. Steeped in private devotional piety, they were not involved in the ritual—they were not praying the Mass.

The liturgical movement came into being to help the baptized reflect the recovered theology of the church and recognize more fully their identity, privileges, and responsibilities as members of the Body of Christ—and to express all this in their liturgical worship, a thing that had not been happening. This was the era of the giants who supplied the theological foundation for the liturgical movement as summed up by Pius X and repeated by subsequent popes: "The primary and indispensable source of the true Christian spirit is active participation in the Sacred Mysteries."

The pioneers of the liturgical movement were Karl Adam, Romano Guardini, Pius Parsch, Louis Bouyer, and the Benedictines in Belgium, Germany, and France. In the United States, in addition to the monks of St. John's Abbey in Minnesota, especially Virgil Michel and Godfrey Diekmann, there were the highly popular and influential authors such as Gerald Ellard, H. A. Reinhold, Martin Hellriegel, and Clem McNaspy, to name but a few.

They saw the theological reason for active participation: the liturgical rites must so engage the participant that they invite a faith-surrender—active participation in its most profound sense. The more the participant responded by a faith-surrender to the sacramental sign, the greater would be the impact of the Spirit on her or his heart, the more intensely would the gifts of faith and love, divine life, be imparted.

During the 1940s and 1950s Gerald Ellard's *Christian Life and Worship* and Clifford Howell's *Of Sacraments and Sacrifice* were both widely read. They stressed the doctrinal foundations for active participation. This phase of the liturgical movement had a solid theology behind it that attempted to relate faith to life through the liturgy. It was a period of much ferment. There were many successes, and the suggestions of liturgists were for the most part welcomed by the people when informed pastors like Msgr. Hellriegel in St. Louis and Msgr. Hillenbrand in Chicago preached and catechized about the need for and the purpose of liturgical renewal.

The task of renewing the liturgy involved two distinct elements. The main goal was to preach the good news contained in the mystery of the Mystical Body of Christ. This would put people in touch with the essentials of the eucharistic mystery. The second goal was to make the liturgy itself more intelligible. That would facilitate their active participation in the ritual.

One of the early attempts to bridge the gulf between the people in the pews and the official liturgy and to get them involved consisted in distributing vernacular missals so the texts the priest read at the altar would be available to them. The goal was to get people to pray and sing the Mass *itself,* not merely pray their private devotions *at* Mass.

The people became more active in the Mass using these vernacular missals and through dialogue Masses, in which the congregation made the responses formerly reserved for the altar servers. Priests tried to get the people to enter into Christ's sacrifice by instituting offertory processions, and by encouraging them to "put themselves on the paten"—and, most important, by more frequent reception of holy communion. There were also attempts to encourage the preaching of the doctrine of the Mystical Body along with all its social implications. While many circles of priests picked up on this, it did not really penetrate the mainstream.

As the church accepted the insights that liturgical scholars and pastoral theologians had been writing about over the forty years preceding Vatican II, the stage was set for the momentous changes that the Council approved. The people welcomed the vernacular liturgy, and it was now possible to solicit their collaboration in worship more directly. Suddenly what had been true only in avant-garde parishes—singing congregations and the participation of laypeople at all levels in the liturgy—became true of Catholicism throughout the Western Church.

Enormous energy on the part of scholars, pastors, and musicians went into producing congregations that actively participated in the Mass. It was a striking accomplishment. The Mass was no longer one devotion among many or a place where one could practice private devotions. It was now seen as the center of Catholic life. The new liturgical forms enabled people, if they wished, to make the Mass their communal prayer and invited their collaboration. This was a grace-filled moment for the church, a source of much vitality.

Liturgists did not focus on people's prayer practices outside the liturgy. Their focus was on the vital need for liturgical reforms. Meanwhile, the renewal of spirituality began in the late 1960s and early 1970s with a revival of interest in directed retreats where the focus was on private prayer.

The spirituality renewal began after the liturgical reforms and long after the theological and liturgical discussions that preceded them. For many the directed retreat was their introduction to a spirituality that delighted and challenged them and awakened in them a thirst for prayer. The focus of the renewal was primarily on one's private prayer life. With its emphasis on decision making and discernment, it helped many people find God's will for them. This renewal of spirituality produced tremendous good for the church and individual Christians.

The directed retreat was not a new concept, however. In fact, its origins can be traced to the late Middle Ages when the liturgy was in a state of decline. The cult of the saints competed with the Eucharist. Saints' feasts invaded the temporal cycle, and long hymns called sequences were sung reciting legends of their lives—there were over a hundred in the missal of the time. The monastic offices had multiplied until community prayers took up most of the day.

In this period of liturgical superficiality a powerful spiritual movement began, the *Devotio Moderna.* It focused on the interior life and individual piety, which were being smothered by excessive communal and liturgical prayer forms. It sprang from earlier reform movements in the monastic and mendicant orders. But it did not close the chasm that existed between the individual's search for God and the official eucharistic liturgy. The Eucharist became one means among many to encounter the Lord, and it was not experienced as a very effective one. It was honored but not integrated.

The new religious congregations that began at this time were strongly influenced by this movement. The Carmelite reformer St. Teresa of Avila was a typical example with her central focus on inner piety, meditation, and private prayer as the path to God. She was questioned by the Inquisition in a way that captures the problem well. She seemed to be challenging the value of sacramental piety and the church's communal worship—the church appeared unnecessary, and the Eucharist was rarely mentioned.

This was not the first time that spirituality and liturgy had taken parallel paths. Some see the first signs of this split in the late third and fourth centuries. After the great persecutions ended many entered the church, some for the wrong reasons. Christianity had become a cultural phenomenon. Some found they could no longer find God in the urban church and its eucharistic assemblies, now compromised by values from a culture alien to the gospel. They went to live apart in the deserts nearby.

Why had the Eucharist lost its power to bring about a dynamic encounter between Christ and the Christian? Was it due to the cessation of persecution and martyrdom? Had the constant threat of death guaranteed commitment to the faith by those who participated in the eucharistic ritual? Once Christianity entered the cultural mainstream, the decision to be a Christian lost its danger and challenge. Did this take away the sense of committed community that had once been there, and that was the necessary context for an intense individual experience of God at the Eucharist? Was the behavior of superficial Christians too distracting?

The community experience of the Eucharist no longer gave some Christians what they needed to guide their daily lives along the path of gospel spirituality, and many of those eager to find God searched for him in the privacy of their homes apart from the liturgy of the church.

In the desert, the liturgy was not essential for many of the Egyptian monks and solitaries. Some, like Anthony, felt compelled to abandon it completely for long periods as they concentrated on their personal struggle with temptation. Pachomius learned the practices that led to perfection from an old hermit: daily fasts in summer, food every other day in winter, nothing but bread and salt, vigils half the night, and often the whole night spent in prayer and meditation. Some took as their model not one of the apostles, or even the Lord in his public life, but the prophet Elijah, who was believed to have lived with his disciples in the caves on Mount Carmel.

This period saw the birth of a highly developed spirituality. Expertise in directing others became a valued skill. New literature on spirituality and spiritual direction came pouring forth from the desert fathers and gave advice on how to encounter God. The Eucharist played only a minor role in these writings.

The most blessed accomplishment of the desert movement was a sharpened skill in dealing with the subtle illusions that block our authentic encounter with God, including the impulse to self-effort that bedevils the pilgrim on his or her journey. Unfortunately, its focus on personal sanctity through contemplation led some to denigrate the active, apostolic life and failed to integrate the Eucharist.

In the following centuries the writings of the desert fathers had a vast and healthy impact on spirituality that was constantly threatened by its exaggerated focus on the individual, as this extreme example reveals:

> Sit in your cell, as in Paradise; leave all memory of the world behind you; watch your thoughts, as a good fisherman watches the fish. Salvation consists in the chanting of psalms; do not abandon it. Remain always in fear and trembling, in the presence of God, like one who stands before an emperor.[1]

Throughout church history this separation between liturgy and spirituality has occurred often. At different times and for a variety of reasons, the liturgy seems to lose its impact. In their search for a larger experience of God, some turn to other paths and the Eucharist is relegated to a secondary place.

It wasn't always this way. In the earliest age of Christianity there is little evidence of any developed approach to personalized spiritual direction. "As far as we can tell, nowhere do the leaders of the community exercise an individual cure of soul. The great concern is the sanctification of the community as a whole."[2] In those earliest centuries people prayed the liturgy. It was the main source of their spiritual life. It was not just community prayer that they were attending. It was their personal prayer.

Unfortunately, the two easily drift apart.

Clifford Longley in an article in *The Times* (London) tells the story of a curious Sufi, a follower of the mystical path in Islam. He had limited knowledge of Christianity, but he began to investigate it carefully. He was baffled by the focus on dogma and even by the presence of a structured church. What most puzzled him was the apparent lack of any systematic mystical pathway.

After much study the Sufi concluded, to his surprise and satisfaction, that this was the most mystical of all the religions. Longley recounts the Sufi's insight: "It did not have a mystical side to it, as other religions do: it was itself a mystical pathway. The 'course of instruction' in mysticism was nothing else but the annual cycle of the Christian calendar, reaching its climax in Lent, Holy Week, and Easter."

Longley comments that the Sufi's insight into Christianity

> was perhaps greater than many Christians', for he had seen the logic behind the rotating pattern of the seasons and festivals, and the logic behind the church's ancient demand that its members should participate in this pattern by regular worship throughout the year, a logic which is not greatly appreciated by Christians themselves.[3]

After all, who comes to Sunday Mass to receive instruction in mysticism?

Longley sees that Christ is the personal mystical master for each of us: "The central idea of Christian mysticism is that Christ is mysteriously able to reach and teach his disciples even though he is not present in the ordinary physical sense that a guru would present."

This strange combination of mystical and liturgical vocabulary was at the center of the vision of Louis Bouyer, one of the earliest leaders of the modern liturgical movement. From his study of the fathers of the church he insisted that "mysticism is always the experience of an invisible objective world into which we enter, ontologically, through the liturgy, through the same Jesus Christ ever present in the Church."[4]

In the liturgical renewal the community experience has been so stressed that the needs of the individual within the community have often been overlooked. After an overly transcendent approach to liturgy, it was refreshing to move in the direction of the horizontal and communal. Unfortunately, there was the usual danger of throwing the baby out with the bathwater. We believe that God intervenes in human history, and it is this intervention that we celebrate in our liturgy. But this intervention in history occurs by an intervention in the lives of each of many individuals. The heavily horizontal and communitarian approach to celebration tended to ignore that the experience of God, while it has to be communal, must also be personal. The experience of being forgiven by God must occur in each person individually.

There is sufficient evidence that the liturgical movement did not satisfy the deepest needs of the Christian people for an experience of God. Today many Catholics look for that experience in other places, such as directed retreats, cursillos, and even Eastern mysticism. The possibility of uniting personal piety with liturgical piety has faded into the background. It is precisely here that the spirituality presented in this book can suggest a corrective and in so doing bring a new depth to liturgical renewal.

Through the centuries, the church has used the New Testament writings as the criterion for its way of life. It has accepted those writings as divinely inspired guides to what its relationship with God should be. Does the New Testament period give us any clues on how to rediscover the unity of Christian liturgy and Christian spirituality? Do these texts give us any indication of the connection Jesus saw between them?

Jesus began his public teaching with the news about the kingdom of God: "It is near." Something new was at hand, which the New Jerusalem Bible calls an "act of supreme intervention." Jesus then detailed the disposition necessary for those who wish to be a part of this kingdom event: "Believe!" He did not invite his hearers to consider proofs or to look at evidence, but to trust his witness.

Trusting a witness without demanding proof, evidence, or signs signals a break with our preferred pattern of operating. Rather than trust groundlessly, we prefer to explore the evidence carefully and reach our own conclusions. Jesus describes trusting without evidence as *metanoia,* a whole new mind-set.

He initiates this process of change by commanding his hearers to love: to love God wholeheartedly and to love the neighbor as the self. He says we must love others as he himself loves and that we must even love our enemies and forgive them from our hearts. These are the opening steps on the journey. But it will not appear to be an easy journey. Jesus repeatedly points out to the disciples their failure to love. His efforts to make them honest about their lack of love and faith is a single thread that runs through his training of his disciples. Their very lack of faith and love, however, if acknowledged, opens the door to childlike prayer, the prayer of petition. It is the mind-set of the child that Jesus urges them to adopt.

He gives them a commandment that cannot be "done" without divine intervention. He drills them to be honest about their inabilities. He teaches them to ask God to intervene in their lives, not in visible successes, but by enlarging their hearts with gifts of love and faith.

This then is the dynamic that operates in Jesus' spirituality. We have outlined his spiritual agenda. But notice that we have not yet mentioned the Eucharist. Will the Inquisitor ask us as he asked St. Teresa, "Have you found a path to God that bypasses the Eucharist?"

Why *did* Jesus institute a ritual and make it an essential element in his spirituality? Like the prophets who preceded him, he was aware of how easily ritual becomes lip service.

Jesus' decision to formulate a ritual can only be understood if we explore the context in which he made that decision. Can we get into Jesus' mind-set? Can we know what he was doing by creating a ritual? What made him do this when he knew how easily ritual performance can push the Love Command onto the periphery? Why did Jesus regard this rite as necessary?

In the next four chapters we will explore the mind-set behind that decision. First, we look at Jesus' awareness of the Father's desires for the world. The decision to ritualize involves Jesus in another decision that God had made long before the Last Supper, way back in human history. It is not surprising that to understand the link between the Eucharist and spirituality, we must go to the fundamentals of human existence, in the very heart of God, into God's experience of the human story. If we are to grasp the Eucharist, we must focus on those elements in humanity that we tend to avoid. They are God's primary focus. That very same focus became the seedbed of Jesus' decision to give us the ritual of the Eucharist.

Chapter Two

"Something Went Wrong"

It was only in the 1960s that we had our first look at Earth from a distance. What we saw looked like a blue marble with white swirls. It looked so fragile and so promising, a bright white and blue island floating in dark space.

Let us come down closer to our "island," as close as an airplane landing at Santa Cruz airport in Bombay. As we approach over the waters of the bay, a swamp rises beneath us. Then there is a hill of sorts, a hill of mud. As we descend, we see things crawling on that mud-hill. Buglike forms slither in and out. People! People are walking between huts. The hill is crawling. Every square foot is occupied. A little child is in a lane between huts; hundreds of people go in and out of endless rows of huts. Then we land, and the vision is past.

On the other side of the airport, as we pass in a bus from the domestic to the international terminal, there's a long stretch with huts all along the roadside. Suddenly a burned-out section appears. Here inches-high borders separate the family spaces, and people still sit where their homes once stood. Between the borders of the burned-out huts, the children still play in the drab lanes without a hint of green. It looks like a chess game with people as the pieces, set out on carefully drawn squares.

The beauty of God's creation of that blue marble in the sky contrasts sharply with the horror of what we are doing to it. Something is out of whack. This is exactly the question raised by one of the priests in the play *Stand-up Tragedy* when he boils the Catholic religion down to three statements: "God made us. Something went wrong. What are we going to do about it?"

Something went wrong. So many of the tales we tell of our beginnings are efforts to explain just what it was that went wrong. The fact that something went wrong is obvious. How does God feel as he gazes at this scene? How can we get at the feelings in God's heart? Is there really an omnipotent God gazing at this horror? Is his everlasting peace unruffled? Is God a passive spectator off in heaven, like the Deist god who created us and then left us to fend for ourselves?

The gaze of the biblical God is fixed on the suffering of human beings created in the image of God. God cannot close his eyes before the horror. He is sleepless. The experience of God before human suffering must be similar to that of a mother watching helplessly as the belly of her starving child swells. She wants to console the child, but she has no words to explain this evil and its causes. Perhaps the greatest pain of a mother of a sick or starving child is knowing that money for food or medicine is available but will not be given.

Of course we, who do not suffer so, may observe that causes and solutions of such injustice are complicated, that things are not as simple as they seem at first glance. We have ways to explain not helping, and ways to absolve ourselves. But to the father of a starving child, things are simple. His child is dying. Money that others could easily afford to give would save the life of the child. Surely they would not refuse. But the father knows they will.

God can remain silent in many areas that touch human existence but one: in the face of human suffering, God cannot remain silent without alienating us, for we will bitterly interpret such silence as a lack of divine love. So God must enter into dialogue with us about evil. For God it is a painful conversation. It focuses on the costly giving away of all God has, including the only beloved Son, God's other self. The agony of entering that conversation is as painful for God as it is for the mother of a starving child. Entering into painful dialogue to explain evil is not an experience God ever wanted or intended.

The prophets of the covenant with Israel claimed to be God's own spokespersons. "Not just knowledge was given to the prophet," Gerhard von Rad notes, "but the feelings in God's heart: wrath, love, sorrow, revulsion, and even doubt as to what to do and how to do it. Something of Yahweh's own emotion passed over into the prophet's psyche and filled it to bursting point."[1]

Israel's prophets often played upon the horrifying. In a striking passage, Jeremiah pictures God turning to the heavens and inviting them to be horrified at what is happening:

> You heavens,
> stand aghast at this,
> horrified, utterly appalled. (Jer 2:12 *NJB*)

Impelled by the prophetic spirit, Jeremiah describes his own experience as he watches Israel's agony:

> The wounds of the daughter of my people wound me too,
> all looks dark to me, horror grips me.
> Is there no balm in Gilead anymore?
> Is there no doctor? (Jer 8:21, 22a)

Why should we look at scenes that horrify us? Because God himself invites us to look at the real, to look at it with him beside us.

In our sweep of our island globe, we now close in on a hillside near Manila. At first a swirling fog hides it. As we draw nearer, we see figures moving about. Coming closer, we see children on a garbage pile. It isn't fog. It is smoke. The garbage heap is smoldering. The children are scavenging quickly. They are good at it, experienced.

Now we are in the Middle East. Young boys walk ahead of an army. They are human minesweepers.

Now we are at a camp in the Sudan. Only the weakest children can be fed. When their weight reaches normal range, they are sent out of the camp; they now stand outside looking in. Only very weak children qualify for the daily gruel feedings. Many are also coming down with pneumonia; coughs and wheezing punctuate their chatter as they wait in line for their gruel. Sometimes photographers from foreign countries come to take pictures of the bloated stomachs and outstretched hands.

In some places people disappear, as in Argentina under the junta. The verb "to disappear" has become a noun: *los desaparecidos.* Violent hands grab them, pummel them, batter them, break their teeth, gouge out their eyes, pull out their nails. This happens to tens of thousands of people, even in countries said to be at peace. Sometimes their bodies are found, sometimes not.

A journalist interviews a young fighter: "What keeps you going?" "The chance to kill the enemy." We yawn. Another headline: "Thousands killed in Yugoslav fighting." We barely notice.

"They charged in wave after wave," the anchorperson tells us, "until the defenders ran out of ammunition and retreated. Despite heavy enemy fire, they ran up the hill. Hundreds were killed, and at the end they ran over the bodies of their fallen comrades." Then, an ad for perfume airs.

What must God feel watching these scenes of human horror? Children intended for divine friendship are living on a smoking garbage heap, searching like dogs for scraps of food. How far this is from what God had in mind in calling forth human life on Earth! What must God feel seeing a child intended for the glorious dignity of the divine image sent onto a battlefield as a human minesweeper? What must it be like for God to see those endowed with the divine spark living in muddy, subhuman squalor?

It must be similar to the shock God experienced upon finding the body of Abel, slain by his brother Cain: "What have you done!" (Gen 4:10). Such a willful human decision to choose death confronted God, the source and giver of life, with something God never intended.

Faced with such scenes, we try to ignore them, to live as if they aren't there. Would anyone who faced the truth relentlessly be able to function? If we had a realistic awareness of human suffering, of people waking up to horror, would we dare to get out of bed?

If we consider Earth's history, we might plot a slow but sure progress. We see only a continuing success story, an ever-upward spiral. But suppose a visitor from outer space came to Earth today. The visitor might well question such "progress" upon observing the lethal combination of brilliant invention and savagery that destroys millions in wars.

Doris Lessing imagines such a visitor, who sees Earth as "a squalid and unsatisfactory planet full of brutes who could be relied upon for only one thing—to kill each other on one pretext or another at the first opportunity."[2] From outside it is like looking "at a totally crazed species."[3]

Atomic energy is like a monstrous dog we hoped to train, but it keeps straining at its leash. Human hands are planting the seeds of future annihilation each day. Some of our finest minds are paid to plant these seeds, and it is likely that we will reap their harvest someday.

We wake up in the morning, work all day, and come home at night with the threat of nuclear catastrophe like Chernobyl an ever-present backdrop. Even though the Soviet Union is no more, the threat of nuclear proliferation remains and has even increased. We are like a town built downstream from a huge and defective dam.

If we ever were going somewhere glorious, it seems something terrible has happened along the way. That terrible something has invaded our species like a virus, and we see its effects in every new generation.

Why should we look at scenes that horrify us? They make us shudder, shiver. The ordinary reader might feel that: "If this book is really about horror, I would just as soon skip it." Horror is an unpleasant feeling. The prophet Ezekiel describes it accurately with two parallel phrases that capture the elements of horror with precision:

> Many people shall be appalled at you,
> and their kings shall shudder over you in horror,
> …every one of them shall continuously tremble. (Ezek 32:10 *NAB*)

Although trembling and shuddering are not usually pleasant, we generously reward artists like Stephen King who produce these effects in us. As long as it's a story and not real, we get a certain pleasure. We imagine it as real and we shiver. To have such feelings means we are alive.

Other authors try to get us to experience horror to make us do something: they use horror to motivate us to act. Some prophets among us consider it important to present realistic images of what may come. There are TV shows, movies, novels, and science-fiction stories that depict what nuclear destruction would be like. These prophets feel it is good for people to be exposed to the true threat that hangs over us. They think it important to shock us into an awareness of the terrible nuclear reality breathing down our necks. It horrifies us; it fascinates us. We feel helpless before it. If we are lucky, it won't happen in our lifetime.

The young Friedrich Engels, Karl Marx's collaborator, tried to get people to do something about the wretched lives of the poor. Much of his book, *The Condition of the Working Class in England in 1844,* is simple descriptions of what he saw as he walked about in Manchester's less pleasant areas. Here is a typical item: " In one of these courts, right at the entrance where the covered passage ends is a privy without a door. The privy is so dirty that the inhabitants can only enter or leave the court by wading through puddles of stale urine and excrement."[4] Engels was horrified. He knew that to get things changed he had to horrify others.

However, there is a far more disturbing element in our global home. It cloaks its violence. It obscures the connection that links us to the horror inflicted upon our brothers and sisters. Not far from the scenes of starving children and murdered youth are diet resorts for that fortunate third of the human race who use three-quarters of the world's resources. There, even pets have more than enough to eat in a wide variety of flavors. In one place on this exquisite blue marble in the sky, food is heaped up; in another, children, mouths open, hope for food in vain.

The prophet Amos thundered against "those ensconced so snugly in Zion" (Amos 6:1). Ancient Israel lived out its history under the prophets' constant threats of coming destruction.

> Your land is desolate, your towns burned down,
> your fields—strangers lay them waste before your eyes;
> all is desolation, as after the fall of Sodom. (Isa 1:7)

The prophets preach images of terror, the day of Yahweh, a day of doom, because people's lives are filled with selfishness, and the needy are trampled underfoot. A day of vengeance approaches.

> The man of high estate will be tinder,
> his handiwork a spark.
> Both will burn together
> and no one put them out. (Isa 1:31)

Even the chosen people are greedy, rebellious, unjust:

> Their insolent airs bear witness against them;
> they parade their sin like Sodom.

> To their own undoing, they do not hide it.
> They are preparing their own downfall. (Isa 3:9)

The prophet, disgusted at their behavior, invites them to look at themselves honestly. With dreadful warnings, he invites them to see where their behavior is leading: "By what right do you crush my people and grind the faces of the poor?" (Isa 3:15).

Even now the human scene has not changed. We face the same threat in our future. We use whatever we can lay our hands on against our neighbor. It is not that the people who lived in the times of the prophets were exceptionally bad. Not at all. What the prophets describe is a large part of the human condition: savagery toward the weak and a ruthlessly competitive way of life that moves along a path of self-destruction.

Into our most civilized scenes come pictures of starving children. But they are not *our* children. They are far away. Occasionally, we see their faces for a minute or two between ads for computers or skin creams. More often, such images never reach our television screens.

> They know nothing of fair dealing...
> they cram their palaces full by harshness and extortion. (Amos 3:10)

> Listen to this word, you cows of Bashan
> living in the mountain of Samaria,
> oppressing the needy, crushing the poor....(Amos 4:1)

> The days are coming to you now
> when you will be dragged out with hooks,
> the very last of you with prongs. (Amos 4:2)

The image of impending destruction runs through the prophet's message. His pictures are intended to frighten, much as some contemporary artists try to alert us to the precipice on whose edge we stand.

These texts are not our favorites. They are never emblazoned on church banners. Such banners are filled with the positive, the assuring, the pacifying. We don't favor prophets of doom. Our Jesus is friendly and smiling. Our crucifix has become smooth and unbloodied. The wounds in Jesus' palms have become rubies. We slumber in a world apart. But the heavenly Father slumbers not. He cannot sleep. He gazes with open eyes at the horror that grips the lives of so many of his children. He invites us to stand at his right hand and to look open-eyed at what he sees—the suffering that leads him to send his Son to Earth.

Moved by our terrible situation, God makes a decision. Something happens inside of God. The Father who is living, personal, wise, and powerful sets himself a new task, and God's very self is to be spent rescuing his dying people.

And so the human story is crossed by another story, an incredible story, impossible for anyone to believe without the gift of wisdom that God also bestows. Here is the heart of the good news: at the deepest point of despair it can be heard, a promise of divine intervention. God is stepping in personally. The human story is to be invaded. God's story will intersect with human history in a most incredible way.

Literature contains some images that can help us understand what happens when two stories intersect. In Shakespeare's *Hamlet,* Rosencrantz and Guildenstern are two lesser figures whose story is subordinate to Hamlet's. In *Rosencrantz and Guildenstern Are Dead,* Tom Stoppard tells their story. Their lives had meaning, but they were fatally caught up in a greater story, that of Hamlet. Similarly, we are blessedly caught up in God's story.

In *The Sirens of Titan,* Kurt Vonnegut imagines Salo, a traveler from a distant galaxy. Salo is carrying a message to a remote corner of the universe. As he passes near our solar system, his spaceship develops mechanical difficulties, so he lands on Titan, a moon of Saturn, and sends word back to his galaxy at the speed of light. It will take 150,000 Earth years for this message to reach his home, Tralfamadore. Salo waits for a return message, watching Earth through a powerful viewer:

> It was through this viewer that he got his first reply from Tralfamadore. The reply was written on Earth in huge stones on a plain in what is now England. The ruins of the reply still stand, and are known as Stonehenge. The meaning of Stonehenge in Tralfamadorian, when viewed from above, is: "Replacement part being rushed with all possible speed."

Stonehenge wasn't the only message Salo had received. There were four others, all written on Earth:

Viewed from above, the Great Wall of China means in Tralfamadorian: "Be patient. We haven't forgotten about you." The Golden House of the Roman Emperor Nero means: "We are doing the best we can." The meaning of the Moscow Kremlin when it was first walled was: "You will be on your way before you know it." The meaning of the Palace of the League of Nations in Geneva is: "Pack up your things and be ready to leave on short notice." Simple arithmetic will reveal that these messages all arrived with speeds considerably in excess of the speed of light. Salo had sent his message of distress home with the speed of light, and it had taken 150,000 years to reach Tralfamadore. He had received a reply from Tralfamadore in less than 50,000 years.

It is grotesque for anyone as primitive as an Earthling to explain how these swift communications were effected. Suffice it to say, in such primitive company, that the Tralfamadorians were able to make certain impulses from the Universal Will echo through the vaulted architecture of the universe at about three times the speed of light. And they were able to focus and modulate these impulses so as to influence creatures far, far away, and inspire them to serve Tralfamadorian ends.[5]

In Vonnegut's tale, Earthlings were in two stories, their own and Salo's. They were being used by a more advanced civilization. In a sense, we are also being used by a more advanced, superior world. We are playing a part in a story we cannot fully grasp even after it is told to us. Our own story is overshadowed by an event outside us that brings a blessing beyond our imagining.

In the novel *2001: A Space Odyssey,* Arthur Clarke imagines human history colliding with a far superior world. In the final chapter he pictures a Star Child coming in contact with Earth and destroying its defense systems with a mere act of will. History as Earth people knew it was ending. The whole meaning of the human story was being transformed by a superior will.

So, too, we are being made the object of the will of Another, of One who is "living, personal, wise, and powerful." We are to become part of a new people, a new race. We will become what we could never make ourselves into. Our destiny intertwines with that of Jesus. Everything new about us is connected to him. Even our awareness of this new way of living comes through him. Somehow, God's will is done through Jesus, and in such a way that we play a blessed part. What God bestows on Jesus is also bestowed on us. Together with Jesus, we become a new creation not of our own doing.

Imagine a squalid village in nineteenth-century Russia. Life there is just bearable. A few elders meet one day and agree on an effort to improve the situation. They will farm the marginal land on free days. The women will sew. The children will scavenge.

Only a handful of families agree to the plan. Most villagers prefer to put up with their lot and to take it easy on their free days. Still, as the weeks and months become years, a very slight change becomes noticeable. The hard workers are getting some extras, a ruble here and there. It provides them with a little more freedom and gives them greater pride in themselves.

Meanwhile, a thousand miles away, unbeknownst to the village, the tsar has decided to mark the coming of age of his son by a spectacular gift. His son begs the tsar to use the gift to help this little village because his nanny came from there.

The villagers do not yet know it, but their lives are about to be invaded by a spectacular act of kindness from outside. They are about to be drawn into another story, one they will find hard to believe.

Whether the villagers like it or not, they have become part of another story. Now, what *they* can accomplish by their own efforts is no longer decisive for their lives. Rather, all depends on how they respond to the coming gift, how they relate to what the tsar has decided.

The villagers first learn of the tsar's decision not because the gift arrives, but because a messenger comes with a proclamation outlining what the tsar has decided and how the villagers can prepare to receive it. Because of this proclamation, the villagers may turn toward or away from the will of the tsar, but they cannot live apart from it. They cannot pretend they are living in another village or turn the clock back.

We also live under the shadow of a decision made by God, apart from us. St. Paul pictures God making that decision in secret, from eternity (Eph 1:3–14). The ages unfold, and no one but God knows of it. But in the fullness of time, God reveals to us this innermost secret of the divine heart—in Jesus. Collective and individual human history is now lived in relation to God's gracious decision to save. We can turn toward that divine will or away from it, but we cannot stand outside it.

Edwin Markham wrote a poem on love:

> He drew a circle that shut me out
> Heretic, rebel, a thing to flout!
> But love and I had the wit to win:
> We drew a circle that took him in.[6]

Our history is now based on that superior "wit" of God, who has drawn a circle that takes us in. God's determination is filled with such deep affection for us that we can scarcely believe it. The Father has, for his own reasons, chosen to gather and transform us, no matter the great cost to himself.

As an artist put it in the mouth of an old woman of the roads:

> It's His work, it's God's great work that is done,
> Afore time was He thought it,
> And as He built the world
> He built His own hurt into the walls of it,
> For mortar to hold the walls to stand forever....
>
> So it is, ...that already,
> Little as they may know it,
> He hath all men taken in His net.
> And when He will He may hale in,
> To bring us all home.
> How else? Shall that Strong One fail of His purpose?
> Or that wise, who makes all, be mistook?[7]

In the world, the Son will experience the divine ache that his Father had felt in building it. His inner life will be taken up with the very painful aspects of human life on Earth, the unshakeable assurance of the Father's unflinching gaze and his intense determination to share his glory.

The conviction that God is concerned and cannot turn away from the suffering of his children is a vital grace for anyone who preaches the gospel, regardless of the season of the year or the texts for that day.

H. A. Reinhold vividly expresses this conviction:

The poor at my side must be an alarm to me. If the colored parish-
ioners are discriminated against, the sacrament must inflame me.
The beauty of the liturgy and its sacred order must be a thorn in
my side if at the same time the socio-economic order of my coun-
try is a mockery of the Gospel and if Christ's friends, the poor, are
ignored while the well-washed, well-dressed, well-housed and
respected are given practical preference as the "good Catholics."[8]

Chapter Three

Jesus Gazes at the World

The Word of God becomes human. When God gazes at the Earth, there is now on its curved surface a human will open to hearing what God wants to say.

As he matures, Jesus becomes conscious that his Father has an agenda. In the Gospels, one of his first words is "business": God has business, an agenda, and Jesus is eager to be a part of it. The decision of the Father preoccupies Jesus. His attention is riveted on it, that "event in God" that created human history. He experiences his own life flowing from it. His delight is in the loving plan of the One he calls "Abba." The heart of Jesus fills to the bursting point.

Jesus imagines the Father gazing at the plight of his children and agonizing about what to do. The gracious decision of God must be revealed to the world. What has been secret from the foundation of the world must be made known.

The news must be told to the helpless: "Little child playing in the slime, rejected by the builders of this human world, do not fear the meaninglessness you are forced to live in. You have justice and wisdom and sanctification and redemption. For you is prepared something never seen nor heard nor even imagined. A divine willfulness is invading your story. Someone with great power is thoroughly shaken at your plight. Unfailing consolation, God's own Spirit, seeks to enter your heart. It will help you recognize the gifts intended for you. There is Someone who cannot sleep while you suffer."

The boy in the smoke of the garbage heaps will be "endowed with the strength needed to stand fast, even to endure joyfully whatever may come" (Col 1:11). God has so decided.

> He raises the needy from the dust;
>> from the ash heap he lifts up the poor,
> To seat them with nobles
>> and make a glorious throne their heritage. (1 Sam 2:8)

Love imagines this boy at a great banquet, a banquet that alone can give meaning to our human story. God's mighty will has decreed: every man, woman, and child will become whole in Christ (Col 1:28). Each is to be raised up in company with Christ, in table fellowship with him (Col 3:1). That includes the boy on the garbage heap.

The book of life has been opened in the presence of the Ancient One, and a name is written there, the name of a starving girl in the Sudan. She is to be born again into God's own story and given "an imperishable inheritance, incapable of fading or defilement" (1 Pet 1:4).

The woman at the end of her resources is destined for fullness of loving, for adoption into the Godhead. The good news is that "you are the object of a plan that God has long ago decreed in Christ. God's own self is coming to full expression in a giving away; such is God's pleasure. Into this divine onrush you will be swept up."

Jesus appeared in Galilee proclaiming the good news about God, a radically new teaching. He used parables to suggest how God deals with the world:

> A great king decided to give a banquet for his son's wedding. He invited all the royal relatives and all the high officials of the kingdom. But he wanted it to be a very special event. So he sent invitations to all the townspeople, and to all the farmers and their families.
>
> He asked the man in charge of the banquet, "Is the banquet hall going to be crowded?" "Oh, no. There will still be room for more, sir."

> Then the king said, "Go into the alleys and the open roads,
> and go behind the hedgerows and into the ditches, and get every-
> one you meet to come. Because I want my banquet hall full."
> (Based on Matt 22:2 ff.)

Imagine people living in an alley or a hedgerow. Optimists, as the day begins they imagine the delicious crust of bread that the baker will throw their way. Then what? Something will come along.

What comes along is beyond their dreams. Their imaginations are too realistic. They expect little from life. Their hopes have long been crippled by past experience. Even their optimism is really despair compared to what is about to happen. When the uniformed servants come to escort them to the royal banquet, will they be able to believe it? Will they take the risk and go with them? Their story with its shabby ups and downs is being drawn into another story, one of a spectacular goodness. They now receive bread from the royal bakery.

This is how God deals with us. God needs guests for the royal banquet. Reckless, even desperate, God doesn't mind who comes, as long as people come. "I want my banquet hall full," God shouts (Luke 14:23). And Jesus is the shout of God.

Jesus conveys for us a royal decision that will transform our life in the alley. Our ability to scrounge will no longer be our source of consolation. We will forget what it is to be hungry. We will never thirst again. Dread of the future will lose its grip on us. We will breathe. This is delightful to hear, but how can anyone believe it?

Jesus is aware that he is our blessing, not just the messenger. He is filled with the assurance of being God's beloved Son. That experience is at the center of his consciousness. He knows himself to be part of another story. In Jesus, God somehow brings us into that story and blesses us for Jesus' sake. The future is no longer a threat. We can live without anxiety today. What is Jesus' inheritance by right becomes ours by God's decision to adopt us.

Jesus preached a God of unexpected goodness, and he used parables to help people imagine such a wonderful God. He took common images and gave them a stunning twist. For example, Jesus used the image of a journey, an image used by many spiritual writers to describe the spiritual life. Sometimes the image involves climbing a mountain. It is our journey toward God. It is an image that focuses on our efforts.

Jesus preached about a journey that is arduous and difficult. But the journey he spoke of was not *our* journeying. God is the traveler who makes the painful effort, pursuing, even rushing after us like a hurrying shepherd in search of a lost sheep.

Here is another image about the extraordinary goodness with which God deals with us:

> There was a factory owner who did not get much business. One day he received a gigantic order. He rushed to the nearest job center to get part-time help. "I will pay double-time," he shouted. It was nine in the morning. At noon he went back, repeated his offer, and got a few more workers.
>
> At four in the afternoon he made a last call, again offering double-time. A few more joined him. At five the work was finished. Everyone lined up to be paid. He told the paymaster, "Give everyone two full days' pay, everyone, even those who only worked a single hour." There would be great joy in many a household that evening at the unexpected bonus. (Based on Matt 20:1–16)

What a strange factory owner! The rules of survival that govern our ordinary way of living in the world are broken: instead of a paycheck for the hours put in, we get a generous bonus. Jesus hoped to delight his hearers with such good news, but he did not try to prove that it was true. He affirmed it and he assured people that God was actually splendidly generous in his gift giving. He hoped people would recognize it to be true. He hoped they would believe it.

How can anyone believe in such splendid news? Life is such a painful struggle. In the parable of the little village in Russia, if the tsar had really decided to give them all that wealth, why do they see only a messenger? Where are the bags of gold? In the story they are between the announcement of the decision and the arrival of the gold. We are in such a situation throughout our lives on Earth. We live in the time of God's promise, when faith alone can keep us in touch with the actual fulfillment of the promise.

What do the villagers have before the arrival of the gold? They have the word of a messenger who has assured them that the money will soon be theirs. Some of the villagers may believe and begin living off that future wealth. Just as a lottery winner starts spending the money she has in the belief that she will soon have more than enough, so some villagers became joyful as soon as they heard the messenger.

Faith that doesn't wait for the appearance of the gold is what Jesus called for: New Testament faith. It means believing with little or nothing of what the world counts as evidence, believing in a promise.

Unfortunately, New Testament faith is often treated as if it were identical with the faith of the covenant with Israel. In discussing what faith means for a Christian, Hebrew Scriptures are often used to explain it. There is a fundamental difference between the two that is easily overlooked. When Jesus placed the promise of an afterlife at the heart of the good news, he radically altered the nature of faith and spirituality. The central promise of Christian faith is about a future event that has no parallel and for which there is no direct evidence. How can such a promise be believed?

In the Hebrew Scriptures, faith in God's promise to help today is made possible by recalling God's faithfulness in the past, preeminently, God's rescue of the Israelites from bondage in Egypt. That past event for which there seemed to be clear evidence was used to summon Israel to trust. Just as God's might was manifest at the Red Sea, it would be manifest in their day. Signs of God's power were expected and sought.

When the Hebrew Scriptures speak of the faith of an individual, he or she also expects evident signs of divine power. God's trustworthiness is going to have to show itself *before* death, and when it does, it will be evident. It is not surprising that the Jews demanded signs from Jesus. For those who believe God is a good God, and who at the same time are convinced there is no afterlife, it is impossible not to expect signs of God's activity on their behalf on this side of the grave: long life, many children, material prosperity.

Not believing in an afterlife has an effect on spirituality too. If we believe there is a God who is putting holiness in our hearts, and if there is no afterlife, we will notice ourselves becoming holier now. If we don't see holiness coming, we wonder, "Does God really love us?" Without evidence that God is bringing us to holiness, how can we enjoy any of God's other gifts? Jesus' opponents were very much into noticing their spiritual strengths and thanking God for them.

Jesus pointed out that you can only notice the noticeable, the measurable. This does not include weightier matters, such as justice, mercy, and love (Matt 23:23). These cannot be measured. As we grow in love, we lose sight of that growth. Our eyes become absorbed in our neighbor's plight. We lose sight of how well *we* are doing.

The followers of Jesus will see the presence of these gifts only in the afterlife. The evidence for their growth in holiness will be given then. Faith in Jesus rests on his word alone and effects a transformation of our consciousness that is a gift of God.

During his agony in the garden, all evidence of God's favor was taken away from Jesus. Yet he chose to trust. By accepting that gift of faith, Jesus was empowered to trust without any signs at all. This decision to trust is the supreme example of Christian faith. All evidence that his mission would be a success was taken from him. But through the power of the Spirit, Jesus opened his heart to the fullness of the gift of faith. That gift enables the believer to share in the divine consciousness.

What are we to do when signs *are* given? What about those situations in which God *does* appear to come through for us? Can't we recall them to help us believe now? For Jesus, such an approach misses the crucial truth: deeper down, God is *always* coming through—that is what the believer knows. The true believer is not caught up in the endlessly changing pattern of events in which God sometimes seems to come through, sometimes seems to do nothing. That is a trap that keeps us on the surface level. Faith plunges deep and touches the ever-active concern of God, a God more concerned for our happiness than we are ourselves, no matter what may appear to happen on the surface.

Jesus calls us to trust that God has made a gracious and irreversible decision to save us. Jesus invites us to live trusting that he tells the truth about God's unswerving will. He assures us that if we trust his Word, we will live in the truth.

This divine and irreversible decision is a spectacular and unprecedented event within God. It is as if suddenly one morning there was a change in the nature of the atom or the speed of light. The effects would be immense and radiate throughout the universe. So too with God's determined will to save the world. That is what Jesus promises: "Fear not; God himself is sleeplessly at work in his determination to save you." Jesus invites us to base our lives on that promise.

How can a mere promise make such a difference? Imagine young Charles, away at boarding school. Christmas is near, and on Friday Charles will go home for two weeks. But on Monday, his mother calls with bad news: Great-Aunt Sophie is ill, and she must go to Paris and stay with her. Charles will have to remain at school for the holiday.

Charles is devastated. After that call, it seems to him that all his fellow students can talk about is going home for the holidays. His teachers tell one dumb joke after another. Classes are dull and boring. Charles is an alien in a world of jollity.

Then on Wednesday, his mother calls again. Great-Aunt Sophie has taken an unexpected turn for the better. Mother will be at school to pick him up on Friday after all.

All Charles has are his mother's words, a promise. But he enjoys school immensely that day. His teachers are witty. Classes challenge him. He has fun with his schoolmates. Even the food tastes better.

Of course, nothing at school has really changed. It is Charles who has been transformed by words of a promise he trusts. He does not wait for Friday to be happy—he is happy now.

One sees a similar phenomenon among lottery winners. All they have is a ticket, a piece of paper. But it's enough. Some even begin to spend the money that is still to come. They trust in the promise, and that's enough to transform their lives. Similarly, the gift of faith lets us experience *now* what the future promises. Those who believe the promises of Jesus find their lives invaded by anticipatory joy.

In one of the parables Jesus describes how it feels to encounter the true God. How does the vagrant feel sitting at the royal banquet clothed in a wedding garment—amazed, embarrassed, incredulous? He is so overjoyed and overwhelmingly grateful, he can hardly believe what is happening.

Here is an image Jesus uses to describe how God behaves toward us:

> The master was due back at ten. Everything was ready. But the hour comes and goes with no sign of him. The servants drift off to bed. Surely the master's staying elsewhere.
>
> But one old woman stays up. "He may yet come." She keeps a low fire and a kettle hot. And at last, he arrives.

> What does the master do? I'll tell you what he will do: he
> will take the apron from around her waist and make her sit down
> to her intense embarrassment and joy. And he will serve her a nice
> cup of tea. (Based on Luke 12:35–37)

Was there ever a master like that? Was there ever a monarch who
searched the hedgerows for table companions?

Jesus assured his listeners that God was their Father. In another
parable he tells his hearers what kind of Father God is.

> There was a rich man in a town who had a wicked son. The son
> would not work or study, and he spent every cent he could get
> from his father. He took to drinking and was insolent to his father.
> Finally, one night, he stole from the cash box and fled. He
> went to a distant town and took to sex and drugs. As the months
> went by, he spent all his money. He begged. He robbed. He was
> arrested. It was either jail, or leave town under escort, so he left
> that place. He decided to go back home. Surely his father would
> not let him starve.
> When he was still way down the road, his father saw him
> coming and ran to meet him. He threw his arms around him and
> kissed him. He ordered the servants to get a ring and a robe and to
> kill the fatted calf for his newly found son. "We must celebrate,"
> he said, "because he is my own son, and he was lost, and now he is
> found. Why, my son was dead, and has come back to life." (Based
> on Luke 15:11–24)

Is this how a father should act? Shouldn't there be some discipline for the boy's sake? Is God really indulgent? For those bowed
down by guilt, this news was a trumpet-summons to life. "Fear not;
your sins are forgiven" (Matt 9:2). God will cut loose the dead weight
of the past. We can become innocent again before him.

In the Gospels, we sometimes see Jesus' response to the crowds:
compassion. Such compassion may seem strange to us, even inappropriate. It is certainly not the feeling we have as we see crowds of shop-
pers in a busy mall or football fans at a televised game.

What did Jesus see in people that we do not? What prompted his
compassion? The Gospels tell us: "As [Jesus] saw the crowds, his heart
was filled with pity for them, because they were worried and helpless"

(Matt 9:36–37). What was the source of their worry? What constituted their helplessness? The emotion of pity seems inappropriate unless Jesus sees something beneath the surface that we do not. Is it something we repress? Does something secretly drain our energy and dictate our choices?

Without knowing it, we are riddled with guilt, lovelessness, and anxiety. Our memory of the past is selective lest guilt overwhelm us. We censor our thoughts of the future and cloak the reality of death lest anxiety paralyze us. Our present existence with its tenacious lovelessness is twisted into "We're OK."

The entire gospel is a response to these basic emotions—guilt, lovelessness and anxiety—that are so threatening we won't even admit them into our consciousness. Jesus sees us, "worried and helpless," harried like shepherdless sheep, abandoned, weighed down with guilt and despair, fearful of what tomorrow might bring, afraid of the death that tomorrow will surely bring. To our guilt for the past Jesus declares: "Your sins are forgiven you" (Luke 7:36–50). To our lovelessness in the present he replies: "Those who drink the water that I will give them will never be thirsty again" (John 4:14). In our anxiety over our future death he assures us: "I am the resurrection and the life…those who believe in me will never die" (John 11:25–26).

Ignatius of Loyola imagined the Trinity looking down on the Earth where "all are going down to hell." Jesus has a similar vision. He is not deceived by superficial cheeriness. He looks at his brothers and sisters in all their competitiveness, injustices, resentment and anger. He sees the joylessness that pervades human life, where protecting ourselves is our first concern. Jesus sees how carefully we hide all this from ourselves. In our mouths are the right words, but our hearts are lost and pitiable.

Jesus was *thoroughly shaken* as he gazed at the human situation. In one of his parables, bystanders report an unforgiving debtor to the king. When we encounter an act of unforgiveness, are we shaken? Not usually. Even when we refuse to forgive within ourselves, we are not troubled by it.

But Jesus is thoroughly shaken. The human situation involves so many illusions, so much turning away from reality. He has compassion because he sees our willful blindness and self-destructive paths. Jesus sees with uncompromised clarity that our destructive course is related to our present unloving choices. He fixes our attention on these choices.

In the Gospels, Jesus' compassion even expressed itself in tears. He wept over Jerusalem on the eve of his passion because of its willful blindness: "Jerusalem, Jerusalem! You kill the prophets and stone the messengers God has sent you! How many times have I wanted to put my arms round all your people, just as a hen gathers her chicks under her wings, but you would not let me" (Matt 23:37).

Another time, Jesus was met by a man filled with evil spirits. No one could keep him chained anymore: "He was too strong for anyone to control him. Day and night he wandered among the tombs and through the hills, screaming and cutting himself with stones" (see Mark 5:4–5). What an apt image for the human condition! Violent forces we cannot control possess us. This story paints a picture of the unredeemed human condition Jesus saw and registers his horror and pity as he sees us on our self-destructive course.

Confronted by self-destructive humanity, Jesus feels compassion. Jesus knows that God has not abandoned us. God is at work in Jesus making up for our inability to cure ourselves. That is what the conclusion to the story of the possessed man affirms: we are in a hopeless situation, but God is working to save us, *and* working effectively.

From the time of his baptism on, Jesus knew he was bound to the human race as an elder brother. He bears within himself a whole new humanity. His pity for men and women is pity for brothers and sisters who are linked to him in a mysterious but real solidarity. It is similar to the compassion we would feel if we discovered that the victim of a car accident we had just passed was not a nameless stranger but a dear relative.

The tears of Jesus before the tomb of Lazarus, the tears of Jesus weeping over Jerusalem's willful blindness, the pity of Jesus for the crowds at large, these are the tears and compassion of God, the everlasting love that moves God to act to save all his children. A substantial amount of Mark's Gospel involves miraculous cures. Jesus sees himself as a physician come to cure the sick, especially the morally sick. To such as these he offers the table fellowship of God's forgiving love. *This* is their cure.

What does God actually do for the people living in the slime and in the mud huts, those gutter-dwelling children? In Jesus, God bestows on us "every spiritual blessing in the heavens." In Jesus, God finds us "holy and blameless," calls us to be "full of love." God bestows on us in Christ a "glorious favor": adoption as God's children, God's heirs (Eph 1:3–14).

As Jesus watched his brothers and sisters leading lives tormented by guilt, despair, and anxiety, he felt God's great pity for them pulsing in his own heart. He felt how important it was for people to know what God had decided to do for them.

> You are foolish and far from true faith. You are slaves of your passions, pulled by pleasures of every kind. Be honest! You go your way in malice and envy, hateful yourselves, and hating one another. But the loving kindness of God is appearing. He has made up his mind to save you, not because of some golden deeds of yours, but because of his mercy. You are to be baptized into a new birth; you are to be made over in the Spirit. You are to become heirs of everlasting life. You can depend on this to be true. (Titus 3:3–8)

There is a story in the Hebrew Scriptures Jesus studied and liked. There was a people headed for destruction because of their wickedness. When God saw this, he was moved with pity. God acted, choosing the prophet Jonah, and sending him to preach the Word of salvation. Jonah met with great success. All the people needed was to hear the truth, even from an alien.

Similarly, Jesus is the great messenger of God's decision to save. He reveals the secret decision of God. In Jesus, all can come to know of the incredible event that took place inside of God before the foundation of the universe. All can hear at last of the glory we are being drawn into—"The innermost heart of God is revealed."[1]

Chapter Four

Jesus the Prophet

God's choice of Israel put the people on the spot. They had to make a choice between two vastly different paths. If Israel accepted God's offer of a special relationship, above all the nations of the Earth, it would enter upon a history of great prosperity, political freedom, and healthy living.

But Israel had the power to refuse God's gift. That was an alternative, thanks to God's particular love. If Israel refused God's offer, its existence would be deeply scarred by the foolishness of that refusal. Like the Russian villagers in the face of the tsar's gift, it was a choice the people could not avoid. They were on the spot.

In Jesus, God offered Israel his only begotten Son, and Jesus was aware of the danger to them. Jesus had to warn Israel of the vital nature of this moment in history. If Israel ignored the lofty, even impossible demands of his commandment to love, any hope of a happy life would be lost. The failure to follow Jesus as he led them to live off the powers of the kingdom would render their lives empty and result in an eternity of pain after death.

Jesus wanted to change people and to get them to make decisions. Their path was leading to destruction. In the Gospels, Jesus sees himself bringing on the end times. There is an urgency in his preaching. He has a task to do that allows for no delay. "Jesus sees men as rushing to their destruction," writes Joachim Jeremias. "Everything is on a knife-edge.

It is the last hour. The respite is running out. He unwearyingly points to the threatening nature of the situation."[1]

Jesus has placed a new element at the center of his promise: everlasting life. God's kind decision is dangerous for the chosen: accept Jesus and know eternal joy, refuse him and know endless pain. To describe the coming catastrophe Jesus uses images designed to make people experience fear and repugnance.

He uses two images repeatedly, fire and darkness. He plants in our minds the image of a "blazing furnace" (Matt 13:42) and warns that people will be thrown into it. A common nightmare is that of being burned alive. Jesus leads us to imagine being burned—not just our fingers, but our whole body. We are used to hearing this image and are perhaps unmoved by it unless an artist makes it come alive for us. Jesus, using his imagination like an artist, tries to dissolve our false confidence. He wants us to realize that a catastrophic future threatens our existence.

The second image Jesus uses often is that of darkness. He threatens his hearers with a future without light. Once again we are in a nightmare world: in a deep, dark forest in the dead of night without any light. "As for the good-for-nothing servant, throw him into the darkness outside, where there will be weeping and grinding of teeth" (Matt 25:30).

Jesus attempts to frighten his hearers, spending much of his imaginative power detailing a terrifying future. With his focus on the demands of the Love Command, Jesus locates our seemingly unimportant decisions in a transcendental setting. By refusing to forgive what we feel is unforgivable, we actually turn our backs on the king's messengers (Matt 22; Luke 14). We climb back down into the ditch.

Jesus often warns his hearers about how surprised they will be. He depicts the wealthy man who decides to build bigger barns and promises himself many years of pleasure. Jesus vividly portrays the man's false confidence. And then the surprise: "Fool! This very night the demand will be made for your soul" (Luke 12:20).

Death is like a skull grinning at the banquet. How easily we ignore it: "It cannot happen." It not only can, but it will unless we change. After all, Jesus' hearers saw themselves as the chosen people, confident of God's special care.

To undermine this deep-rooted confidence, Jesus used *reversal*. For instance, he describes the great Day of Judgment. The moment has arrived when his hearers are called to be judged, and they expect some well-earned praise. Then Jesus depicts a strange interruption. A group of pagans rises up from among the onlookers. Their words will bring about the condemnation of this generation despite their membership in the chosen people. "Assyrians, pagans you have never met, rising up and successfully condemning you. That is what awaits you" (see Matt 12:41). It's an image designed to frighten the chosen.

In another effort to imagine that great Day, Jesus presents the Queen of the South, another pagan who will expose the evil hidden in his hearers' lives (Luke 11:31; Matt 12:42). Jesus even uses the most abominable of all images, Sodom and Gomorrah, and warns his hearers that "it will be more bearable" for the inhabitants of those two cities than for anyone who refuses to listen to his warnings (Matt 10:15).

It was especially difficult for the Law-abiders to take Jesus' warning to heart. Keeping the Law of God was all the security they needed. Jesus called them hypocrites. They did observe the Law in less important matters but ignored "justice and mercy and faith" (Matt 23:23 *NRSV*), straining out a gnat but swallowing a camel (Matt 23:24).

Another human source of confidence comes thinking, "We were there when it all happened," or "We knew him when...." This is the occasion for Jesus to paint another reversal scene. Again we are at the judgment. It is the moment when Jesus is revealed as the Messiah of God, when his contemporaries—"this generation," those who are actually listening to his words—are excluded. They will appeal to their intimacy with him. "We were there when you came. Have you forgotten how close we were? We're not like those others: We were right there, and we ate and drank in your company. It was in our streets that you taught" (see Luke 13:26 ff.). But they will hear the words: "Away from me, you evildoers" (Luke 13:27).

Jesus' imagination fills in the details: weeping, gnashing of teeth, as they watch with disbelief, when "people from east and west, from north and south will come and sit down at the feast" (Luke 13:29) and they themselves are not let in. "You are headed for a terrible surprise. You who are now first will be last" (see Matt 20:16).

Jesus uses reversal over and over again. His hearers will wake up one day, and find that they have been walking straight toward their own doom, and it will be too late to turn back. They will find themselves in a strange landscape. Then they will recognize how blind they have made themselves. Their confidence will suddenly be seen to be without foundation. The cure? "Open your eyes now. Your reasons for confidence are illusory." Isn't this what Michelangelo captures in the despairing face of the damned person in his *Last Judgment,* who realizes too late what the gospel warned us about all our lives? John the Baptist had put it clearly: "Do not presume to tell yourselves 'We have Abraham as our father.'" He then rolled a hand grenade at that defense: "God can raise children of Abraham from these stones" (Matt 3:9).

It was inevitable that false confidence would spring up from closeness to the Messiah, but Jesus repeatedly undermines it. Capernaum was especially difficult—he had spent so much time there. He aims his image with precision: "Do you want to be raised high as heaven? You shall be flung down to hell" (Luke 10:15). In fact, living at the time of the Messiah will prove to be a disaster for many, for that generation has the opportunity to reject him.

> This generation will have to answer for every prophet's blood that has been shed since the foundation of the world, from the blood of Abel to the blood of Zechariah who perished between the altar and the temple. Yes, I tell you, this generation will have to answer for it all. (Luke 11:50–51)

Jesus' disciples feel confident that his warnings are not meant for them. This development is unavoidable and forces him to expend much energy trying to undo it. How can his disciples apply the threats of disaster to themselves when he assures them, "To you is granted to understand the mysteries of the kingdom, but to them it is not granted" (Matt 13:11)? How can they feel fear when they hear him say, "Blessed are your eyes because they see, your ears because they hear. Many prophets...longed to see what you see, and never saw it; to hear what you hear and never heard it" (Matt 13:16–17)?

How can his disciples not feel secure against the threats when they work miracles? Their call to discipleship quickly becomes a protection against reality. In order for the disciples to be able to hear of the future that threatens their lives, they must be stripped of all false confidence. "When the day comes, many will say to me, 'Lord, did we not prophesy in your name, drive out demons in your name, work many miracles in your name?'" (Matt 7:22). Is this not aimed at the miracle-working disciples who rejoice in their powers?

Jesus spells it out so accurately. What must it have been like for the disciples to have their insides laid bare like that? He aims right at their confidence to destroy it: "Then I shall tell them to their faces: I have never known you; away from me, all evildoers" (Matt 7:22–23). It is a fate much worse than that of the crowds, and it threatens the disciples precisely because of their closeness to the Messiah. What could be worse than to hear the words "Away from me" at the judgment?

It is a strange truth, but the closer we get to people, the more vulnerable they become. We have the opportunity to do enormous evils to them, evils we cannot inflict on our enemies. Being a disciple of Jesus brings with it the ability to harm him far more seriously than the crowds ever could. At the same time, being a disciple of Jesus brings with it a subtle assurance that we would never do anything to harm him—and we become oblivious to the increased danger that we might actually do so!

It is to the disciples that Jesus says: "One of you is a devil" (John 6:70). When Jesus reveals that he will die, Peter refuses to accept it and urges Jesus to forget such a depressing possibility. Jesus calls him "Satan" (Matt 16:23). The very assurance, "Nothing really bad can happen," is precisely the reason why Jesus' warnings have had so little effect. Now it is actually urged on Jesus himself by a close disciple. He lashes out: "You have become a tool of Satan."

It was also to Peter, when he asked how often he must forgive, that Jesus spoke the dreadful words: "In his anger the master handed the dishonest steward over to the torturers till he should pay all his debt. And *that* is how my heavenly Father will deal with you" (Matt 18:34–35).

In this parable, Jesus combines the father image that is central to his preaching with the master enraged at the behavior of the servant. The warning is clear: this is one and the same God. In his offer of intimate friendship you are put on the knife's edge. Unless you become keenly aware of this reality now, you will be stunned at the day of judgment.

You will encounter a God you never knew. In place of the indulgent father, you will meet a stranger.

Jesus carved out another vivid image of warning near the end of his public life. "The disciples came and asked him when they were by themselves, 'Tell us when this is going to happen'"(Matt 24:3 ff.). It is in this setting, alone with his disciples, that Jesus describes the great judgment in all its glory: "Come, you whom my Father has blessed" (Matt 25:34). He vividly pictures the scene down to the very words that will be spoken, even the words he himself will be saying: "Go away from me, with your curse upon you, to the eternal fire prepared for the devil and his angels" (Matt 25:41). He was determined to frighten them.

In his interaction with the disciples we can see clearly how Jesus worked to undermine their false sense of security. His primary weapon was the lofty demands of the Love Command. "Do you really love your brothers as you love yourself? Do you actually love your enemies? Do you forgive from your heart those who are unfair to you?"

He pointed out their competitiveness. He deliberately used the word *love* rather than less demanding alternatives: "You must *put up with* your neighbor"; "you must *be courteous* to your enemy"; "you must *treat* people as if you did love them." This is the insight that Jesus points out to Peter in the parable of the unforgiving debtor (Matt 18:23–35). "Unless you forgive your brother and sister from your heart," this image will indeed become your experience: "you will be handed over to the torturer."

In the judgment scene Jesus links this ominous future to their present reluctance to feed the poor, to welcome the stranger, to visit those in prison, to struggle against injustice. He spends so much of his time with the disciples waking them up to those areas of their *present* reality that will, unless checked, lead them away from God.

On one occasion Jesus tries to get at the apparently unimportant but actually vital presence of evil within their hearts. "Keep your eyes open. Look out for the yeast of the Pharisees" (Mark 8:15). Growing secretly, hidden within, is the potential for enormously evil choices. Search for it. Presume it will be there even when it is invisible.

But in that same incident they misinterpret his words, and his exasperation flames out at them: "Do you still not understand, still not realize? Are your minds closed? Have you eyes and do not see? Ears and do not hear?" (Mark 8:17–18). Unlike the crowds to whom Jesus had applied this text from Isaiah, at first the disciples *did* seem to see and hear. But that is no longer the case. "Do you still not realize?" (Matt 16:9).

It is a tongue-lashing, but Jesus feels it is desperately needed. Unless they come to realize that their seemingly unimportant lives are filled with potential for great good and for great evil, all is lost. And he wonders: "When the Son of Man comes, will he find any faith on earth?" (Luke 18:8). To be standing near when he spoke this way was to be invited to a strange picture of reality. Those closest to him are in enormous danger precisely because of their closeness. But this is hidden from them and its likelihood is ignored.

There are those in our day who claim that modern people cannot hear the warnings of Jesus, that our culture makes it impossible for us to take them seriously. The presupposition seems to be that it was otherwise in Jesus' day. But in the Gospels nothing is plainer than the reluctance of the disciples to hear what Jesus was saying.

A most powerful warning is given in yet another depiction of the Great Judgment. "Anyone who disowns me in the presence of human beings, will be disowned in the presence of God's angels" (Luke 12:9). Jesus will disown the one who disowns him. Again listen to Jesus: "If anyone is ashamed of me and my words, of him the Son of Man will be ashamed when he comes in his own glory, and in the glory of the Father and the holy angels" (Luke 9:26).

"If that happens, I will be ashamed of you." It is a side of Jesus that they must not see at the Judgment. Now he warns them: "It is indeed a part of me." What an image for the disciple: a Messiah who is ashamed of him. How did they feel as they listened? It was all unreal, unlikely: "After the psalms had been sung they left for the Mount of Olives, and Jesus said to them, 'You will all fall away from me tonight'" (Matt 26:30–31). Instead of reacting with horror, they reject it as unreal. Peter leads the way: "I will never fall away."

It is then that Jesus raises before Peter an even more staggering possibility: "You will disown me three times." Peter rejects the warning. His self-image does not admit the possibility. His denying the Lord is so unlikely that it seems unreal, not worth considering, not even worth preparing himself against. The exchange is a miniature of human reaction to Jesus' words of warning, the vast confidence that none of this refers to us. Peter insists: "I will lay down my life for you" (John 13:37). How certain he is!

Jesus replies like a mother to her naive child, "You will lay down your life for me, will you?" He invites Peter to see himself as he really is, to enter the real world where he is becoming one of the cowards who will deny their Lord.

"One of you is about to betray me" (Matt 26:21). The words shake them. Perhaps Jesus' saying "Someone who has dipped his hand into the dish with me will betray me" calls to mind images of betrayal that they know well:

> Even my friend who had my trust
> and partook of my bread,
> has raised his heel against me. (Ps 41:9)

> If an enemy had reviled me,
> I could have borne it.
> …But you, my other self,
> my companion and my bosom friend.
> You, whose comradeship I enjoyed;
> at whose side I walked in procession
> in the house of God. (Ps 55:12–14)

Here is *the* most unwelcome image, the betrayal of the long-awaited Messiah by one of those closest to him. We are used to it, but it unnerved the disciples. They no longer reject it immediately, but ask, "Surely it is not I, Lord?" Throwing the image aside, Peter speaks: "Even if I have to die with you, I will never disown you" (Matt 26:35). And all the disciples say the same thing.

Toward the end of the supper, they affirm their faith in him: "We believe that you come from God." Jesus answered them, "Do you believe at last?" (John 16:31). He then repeats the same warning: "Listen: the time will come, indeed it has come already, when you are going to be scattered, each going his own way and leaving me alone" (John 16:32).

St. Ignatius, seeking to help the retreatant experience shame, suggests a similar image in his *Spiritual Exercises:* "[That] of a knight brought before his king and the whole court, filled with shame and confusion for having grievously offended his lord from whom he had formerly received many gifts and favors."[2]

There is glory and catastrophe hidden within humdrum human relationships. We relate to God precisely as we relate to others. The greatest intimacy with God is ours to choose—and so is the alternative of betraying him. One of them is our future.

The saints explored this world and were most familiar with it. Ever present to them was the monstrous possibility. As that most happy saint, Philip Neri, prayed, "Lord, do not trust Philip, for he will betray you."

Feelings of horror are part of the Christian experience. Love for the poor and the oppressed makes us share their existence. Jesus warned of the future that awaits those who do not feed the poor, of the millstone around the neck and drowning for those who scandalize little children.

Jesus saw people marching toward destruction. He saw within them an unforgiving lovelessness that calls for "being handed over to torturers" (Matt 18:34–35). He warned those who are drawn so powerfully by the magnet of their passions that they are deaf to his voice. Today, we remain a "crazed species," living apart from the truth, in a bubble of illusion, like the "warped and crooked generation" (Phil 2:15) of which St. Paul wrote.

Jesus sees us bowed down by care and threatened by death. He comes into that darkness in which we live, in which we compete with each other and worry about overeating while ignoring our starving neighbor, and he finds injustice deeply embedded in our social structures.

Chapter Five

Jesus Ritualizes

To enter into Jesus' mind-set is a very murky undertaking, but the effort to do so has been present ever since the apostles first looked back at their time with Jesus. They tried to "get inside his head," to grasp the human experience that was within.

In their "memoirs" they present his public years as leading toward a moment of supreme choice. Jesus' life moves toward the fullness of decision, a choice in which he will define himself completely.

Some factors are clearly present. Fundamental to this moment is Jesus' conviction that he is the intersection of two worlds: into our history comes a kingdom that is not of this world. It is similar to what some astronomers see when they observe two galaxies colliding, or when science-fiction writers portray a superior civilization making its power felt in the human story.

A second factor is the collapse of any hopes Jesus may have had that telling people about this cosmic event would be enough to get them to change their lives and begin living in accord with the reality that was coming to be. Unlike the people of Nineveh who acted on Jonah's word, people Jesus encountered were not open to believing what he said. They wanted signs. Illusion's grip was so powerful that the preaching of the truth had no transforming impact on them. Once people realized that Jesus' message was one of trust in a spectacular action of God that was not immediately apparent, they turned away. They wanted to see the gold then and there.

The extrabiblical *Gospel of Thomas* catches this experience of Jesus in the face of the unbelieving audience to whom he preached: "I stood up in the midst of the world, and I revealed myself to them in the flesh, and I found them all drunk, and I found no one among them who was thirsty; and my soul is in pain over the sons of men, because they are blind in their hearts and see not that they are poor and do not realize their poverty."[1]

And so, God's secret decision to give the Godhead away, his decision to free us from death, guilt, and lovelessness, remained unknown as yet. The people still did not understand the good news of liberation. They had ears, but heard not. The sway of competitiveness and anxiety continued, despite God's decision and Jesus' preaching. Jesus wanted to draw people under his wings, but they chose not to respond.

Did Jesus go into isolation and prayer as he reflected on the failure of his mission? Various texts from the Hebrew Scriptures must have come to his mind. He knew he was the decisive instrument of God for the salvation of the world. What could the failure of his preaching mean? Could it be that the banquet hall would not be filled? "Shall that strong One fail of His purpose? Or that Wise, Who made all, be mistook?"[2] Are all the prophecies to fail? Will God turn away from this world and its crazed species and start again somewhere else? Has the truth become so alien to human beings that nothing can break the grip of illusion?

But God's heart is *still* moved with compassion. God's eyes are *still* fixed on the flock. The Shepherd will not abandon his sheep. God is neither slumbering nor distracted. God's gaze is fixed even more intently on the people, now that they do not recognize the hour of their deliverance. Somehow a way will be found to get past their hardness of heart.

In *Rediscovering the Parables,* Joachim Jeremias describes Jesus' mind-set: "No doubts with regard to his mission can make Jesus waver in his certainty that out of nothing, ignoring all failure, God is carrying his beginnings on to completion."[3]

How was Jesus to play a decisive role when his preaching was futile? Into his memory came a story he had heard and studied many times, first told by the prophet Isaiah many centuries before. He told a tale of a strange hero, a man whom God had used to save his chosen people. Jesus had first heard it in the synagogue on the Sabbath many years before. In their post-resurrection awareness, the disciples heard these words with opened minds as they were read in the synagogue. From the earliest days of the church, the disciples wondered about the impact this tale had on Jesus' thinking (Rom 4:25; 10:16).

> There was in him no stately bearing to make us look at him,
>> nor appearance that would attract us to him.
> He was spurned and avoided by men,
>> a man of suffering, accustomed to infirmity,
> One of those from whom men hid their faces,
>> spurned, and we held him in no esteem.
>
> Yet it was our infirmities that he bore,
>> our sufferings that he endured,
> While we thought of him as stricken,
>> as one smitten by God and afflicted.
> But he was pierced for our offenses,
>> crushed for our sins;
> Upon him was the chastisement that makes us whole,
>> by his stripes we were healed.
> We had all gone astray like sheep,
>> each following his own way;
> But the LORD laid upon him
>> the guilt of us all.
>
> Though he was harshly treated, he submitted
>> and opened not his mouth;
> Like a lamb led to the slaughter
>> or a sheep before the shearers,
>> he was silent and opened not his mouth.
> Oppressed and condemned, he was taken away,
>> and who would have thought any more of his destiny?
> When he was cut off from the land of the living,
>> and smitten for the sin of his people,
> A grave was assigned him among the wicked
>> and a burial place with evildoers,
> Though he had done no wrong
>> nor spoken any falsehood....

If he gives his life as an offering for sin,
> he shall see his descendants in a long life,
> and the will of the LORD shall be accomplished
> > through him.
Because of his affliction,
> he shall see the light in fullness of days;
Through his suffering, my servant shall justify many,
> and their guilt he shall bear.
Therefore I will give him his portion among the great,
> and he shall divide the spoils with the mighty,
Because he surrendered himself to death
> and was counted among the wicked,
And he shall take away the sins of many,
> and win pardon for their offenses. (Isa 53:2–12)

It is indeed a very strange story. At its center is one pierced and striped with his own blood, a lamb, innocent and slaughtered. It fits the moment in Jesus' life when there was the threat of violence and the suggestion of murder. Jesus' own death would be at the center of God's way of saving the human race. Somehow, through Jesus' suffering, as with those of the Servant, God would justify many. Somehow, Jesus' death would win pardon for sin and raise a fallen world. Jesus saw in the Servant's death and vindication an invitation to hope despite the failure of his preaching.

In reflecting on these scriptural words, Jesus felt himself invited by his dear Father to suffer. Despite the reluctance he felt in the garden the night before he was to die, Jesus refused to believe that his impending death was a sign that his mission had failed. He knew the Father loved him. He knew he would be the salvation of his brothers and sisters.

This is the great moment in human history. A human mind is receiving a revelation that lays bare the very heart of God. All the elements of Jesus' growing awareness of his being and mission—the threats of death, the Father's love for him and for all, the divine will to save the human race—come together in the Isaian text. Jesus becomes aware that God so loves us that he will not spare the beloved Son.

It has been said that the scriptures were not written for us but for Jesus, to enable him to discover God's secret plan to redeem the world. Scripture also gave Jesus words to express what God was doing in him.

In the words of Isaiah God unfolds for Jesus that secret decision to save the world, and also reveals the terrible price God would pay to do so.

Jesus imagines that terrible price in a parable (Matt 13:24–30). He pictures a field whose owner has the servants plant wheat. The servants are surprised as the seeds sprout, for weeds as well as wheat appear. Something has gone wrong. Where did the weeds come from?

Why, at the banquet of life with more than enough for all, do a few strong ones gorge themselves while others huddle, cold and hungry? God is perplexed. Where did the weeds come from?

"An enemy has done this," the owner decides. Jesus imagines the moment when his Father discovers that he has an enemy. The servants, still hoping for a great harvest, offer to pull up the weeds. But they cannot. The roots of weeds and roots of wheat are intertwined.

"Let them grow together." The separation at the harvest of weeds and wheat will be painful, but there is no other way to save every grain of wheat, not one of which must be lost. The harvest will be great and the granary filled, but before that, a frightful separation must take place.

In the scriptures, Jesus finds suggestions that lead his consciousness into the depths of God's will. We are to be raised up into a glorious story. Our endless competitiveness will not bring catastrophe. Our story will be invaded by another story. All of human history will become a part of this other story. Here is a text that Jesus knew well:

> As I looked, thrones were placed
> and one that was ancient of days took his seat;
> His raiment was white as snow,
> and the hair of his head like pure wool;
> His throne was fiery flames,
> its wheels were burning fire.
> A stream of fire issued and came forth from before him;
> a thousand thousands served him.
> Ten thousand times ten thousand stood before him,
> The court sat in judgment and the books were opened. (Dan 7:9–10)

The prophet is describing an event that takes place in the heavens. He has set the scene. Now the action begins: "I gazed into the visions of the night. And I saw, coming on the clouds of heaven, one like a son of man" (Dan 7:13).

Who is this strange human figure who wanders into the heavenly story? "He came to the One of great age and was led into his presence." Jesus felt invited to see himself as this person:

> On him was conferred sovereignty, glory and kingship,
> and men of all peoples, nations and languages
> become his servants.
> His sovereignty is an eternal sovereignty
> which shall never pass away,
> nor will his empire ever be destroyed. (Dan 7:14)

In texts like this, Jesus found images that enabled him to grasp and express his inner experience. The inner self of Jesus was coming to know a secret that until then only God had known. All that belonged to God, "the One of great age," was being handed to Jesus, the Beloved, the center of human history. The life of Jesus became the arena of the world's fate. Jesus was encountering a divine will immensely more powerful in its loving than any in our human experience. The human family was now linked to him and was being rescued from death and from evil so repulsive that it cannot be looked in the face.

What inner assurances were flooding Jesus' consciousness and enabling him to believe that through him God was definitively entering into the world? According to the theologian Marcus Barth, when Jesus experienced being the Beloved of God, he knew that it was not just that the very self of God was being poured out on him alone. Rather, he saw that in him God effectively loved every human being linked to him by a mysterious solidarity.

Since in God's plan Jesus contains within himself a great people, the election of Jesus is the election of all his brothers and sisters. Our resurrection from death in Jesus is the revelation of that gracious secret hidden in God from eternity. The gospel, then, is nothing but the publication of the secret of the election, God's bold decision to raise Jesus from the dead and us with him.[4]

Once Jesus grasped his death as central, especially through Isaiah's Servant Songs, he had to prepare the disciples for it. His preaching began to center on his death. He drew his disciples apart. He introduced them to his conviction that his death would be used by

God to bring in the kingdom: "Then Jesus began to teach his disciples: 'The Son of Man must suffer much and be rejected by the elders, the chief priests and teachers of the Law. He will be put to death, but three days later he will rise to life'" (Mark 8:31).

In Jerusalem, the coming violence spills into one of his parables: "The only one left to send was the man's own dear son. Last of all, then, he sent his son to the tenants. 'Surely they will respect my son,' he said. But those tenants said to one another, 'This is the owner's son, let's kill him, and the property will be ours!' So they seized the son and killed him and threw his body out of the vineyard" (Mark 12:6–8).

In the midst of the final controversies in the temple, Jesus raises the question of the identity of the Messiah. He interprets a verse of Psalm 110:

> While Jesus was teaching in the temple, he said, "How can the scribes say that the Messiah is the son of David? David himself, by the Holy Spirit, declared, 'The Lord said to my Lord, "Sit at my right hand until I put your enemies under your feet."'" David himself calls him 'Lord'; so how can he be his son?" (Mark 12:35–37)

Is this a text that helped him as he moved deeper into the mystery: "Who am I?"

Another fitting text came to his mind. He was being evaluated and found wanting by the leaders of the people. He had begun to warn them. They were on the verge of committing murder, the murder of the long-awaited Messiah:

> It was the stone rejected by the builders
> that proved to be the keystone;
> This is Yahweh's doing
> and it is wonderful to see. (Ps 118:22–23)

In a sense, Jesus is now speaking for the record. The disciples must be made aware that his death did not surprise him. "No one takes my life from me, because I lay it down of my own accord. I have power to lay it down, and I have power to take it up again" (John 10:18). They must remember that. He would willingly allow his enemies to have their hour.

But his disciples ignored his predictions. His words were met with stony silence. If his own disciples would not believe him despite his special efforts to teach them, how would anybody else ever believe?

Here was a village carpenter who had turned to preaching. He had gathered an odd collection of followers. He was infuriating some powerful people, and he was headed for a violent end. But he believed that this disgraceful end to his career was to be, like Sinai, a high moment of God's full self-disclosure. Unlike Sinai there would be no epiphany, no visible intervention of God, no legions of angels. Its divinity would be hidden.

> But when He really did appear upon the scene
> so other
> so invisible in his divinity
> so unrecognizable
> it was not the kind of otherness and strangeness
> that we had foreseen and expected
> and he thus remained in fact unrecognized.[5]

How can this good news for the whole world, which is embedded in a carpenter's death, be preached to everyone? A way must be found. But even if it is preached, who will believe it?

Jesus sees the next few months of his life as the central moment in human history. A victory of unimaginable importance is about to occur but it might go unnoticed. A way must be found to get the news out. Jesus turned to the power of his imagination. He saw our imaginations as the entry into the human heart. Somewhere in the unfolding of those final months of Jesus' life, he makes a decision based on his knowledge of human nature, a decision to ritualize the salvific event that is central to the two stories, human and divine.

What is behind this decision? It seems so unnecessary, so uncalled for. Why link pure gospel spirituality to a ritual with all the accompanying problems, such as the danger of meaningless formulas repeated by rote. The very word *ritual* is used to describe a repetitious pattern of behavior that has lost its meaning. Just as Jesus' preaching used a series of carefully crafted images of goodness, now a rite becomes central to the intersection of divine and human history.

A way is found to let the gospel shine forth, despite the power of human "wisdom" to conceal and smother it. Jesus decides to express his acceptance of death in ritual eating and drinking. Bread and wine will contain murder and glory. Through our open mouths, we will receive our future. This ritual meal becomes the most effective announcement of the good news. God's eternal decision to graciously favor us is one we can now taste.

What was he hoping for, this ex-carpenter from Nazareth? Why did he choose such a strange path? Often rituals arise in the distant past, in prehistoric times and unknown authors. Their origins lend themselves to reasonable explanations. It is the very nature of the way we are being saved that led Jesus to ritual. There is much to tell his disciples. There is so little time. In fact, there is *too* much to tell them. It is not simply a question of their hearing the truth; it is also a matter of it penetrating them. To go from the ear to the heart takes time, as it does the light of the stars to travel from its source to our sight. The human intellect is little help in finding a path into the human heart.

So Jesus extends an invitation to a ritual banquet at which we eat his body and drink his blood. Somehow in that meal we become what we eat and drink. Joined to his death, we are raised with him to life. Eating and drinking, we enter his story.

In her story of the sacrament of reconciliation, Adrienne von Speyr suggests the mind-set of Jesus when he instituted the rite we used to call confession:

> God stands before God in the attitude that is fitting for God. Analogously, we can designate this as the attitude of confession, since it is the attitude in which God shows himself as he is and since this revelation is expected by God himself....For God it is bliss to reveal himself before God....
>
> In this fashion God stands before himself in the attitude of God, in an attitude perpetually corresponding to and emerging from the perpetual present moment of eternity, in an attitude of trust, of gratitude, of surrender, and of acceptance. When the Son institutes confession at Easter, he does so to bring this divine attitude closer to human beings, to mediate to them part of the Trinitarian life.[6]

That same invitation to share Jesus' relationship with the Father is in the Eucharist. Like the divine Son, we come face to face with the Father. We are invited into his loving surrender to the Father's will. By eating Jesus' flesh and drinking his blood, we are empowered to surrender our will, and we are assured of our adoption. Children of God, we feed on God.

In instituting the Eucharist, Jesus took full account of our lack of faith and love. The eucharistic ritual presupposes this lack. He deliberately chose to leave us a liturgical act that incorporates the giving of faith and love. He attached our reception of faith and love to an external rite. When the moment came for him to go beyond preaching, ritual was the path he took.

When we meet God in the Eucharist, we receive an awareness of God's election of Jesus and of his raising Jesus from the dead. In drinking his blood, we are invited into the intoxication of God's inner consolation. "The love of God is poured into our hearts by the Spirit who is given to us" (Rom 5:5). "Be born again in the faith which is the body of the Lord and in the love which is the blood of Jesus Christ," wrote Ignatius of Antioch in his *Letter to the Trallians*.[7] It is Jesus' faith and Jesus' love that we receive. When we eat his flesh and drink his blood, we receive a share in the trust Jesus has in God and the love Jesus has for his brothers and sisters. As his faith and love are poured into us, our history is being changed.

In the Eucharist God shares the divine consciousness with us. God invades our consciousness and enables us to know what we could never know by ourselves. This is the gift of faith, our coming to know what once only God knew. In the Eucharist we become conscious of God's secret decision to send Jesus as the Beloved Son and to raise Jesus from the dead and us with him. The will that is not loving is made loving and more sensitive to the needs of others, and the will that does not believe starts to believe. Such love and belief are beyond what human nature can produce.

As Godfrey Diekmann, in *The Reform of Catholic Liturgy,* says:

> To the degree that in the liturgical action their personal faith is deepened, their love quickened, to that degree God is glorified....What else can be truly worthy of God except *persons* who

believe more fully, who love God and their fellow men more deeply, and learn to do so in the mass.[8]

Ritual can have two effects. In the imagination it can raise the possibility that life can become eternal joy. In the heart, ritual can be the channel by which the Spirit is poured into the human intellect and will, enabling the participants to believe the good news they have glimpsed in their imagination and to live according to the glory they are approaching.

Because Jesus' salvific death is the event at the very heart of the universe, it will have an effect slowly but surely, as energy moves out from its core to the farthest reaches of the universe in time and space. This outflow occurs as we repeat the rite that is filled with the power of his salvific death, a rite that bridges time and space.

The eucharistic image that Jesus wants to be our central focus, the assimilation of God's very life, is a symbol of endless imaginative power. It dramatically proclaims the fundamental gospel principle that the only stance of a creature before God is receptivity. We are saved through the energy we receive from Jesus. The believer now uses the same energy source that God uses, the Holy Spirit. The Spirit is poured into us through contact with Jesus' glorified body and blood.

What Jesus has done, then, is to make the ritual act a vehicle for the giving of the Spirit. The real presence of the flesh and blood of Jesus, of his glorified humanity, is the instrument God uses to share the divine joy with us.

This ritual meal exerts unavoidable pressure on us to become God's friends, to become God's children, to become like God. We utter that "Abba" that belongs to Jesus alone. We hear words reserved for Jesus. Through the powers of the new age, we join ourselves to Jesus in his decision to surrender his life to the Father. We enter the life of the Trinity united to Jesus the Son. What he inherits, we inherit.

In the Eucharist, Jesus forces us to hear an invitation to be intimate with God. God has died for *us:* we cannot keep our distance. Either God is the heart of our being, or a vast gap yawns between God and us.

In the story of the village, after the tsar's decision, the villagers' lives could have no meaning apart from it. Even if they refused his gift, they would be famous for that refusal. They could no longer stay just in their own story. Former categories of success, such as extra work or discipline, no longer mattered. What became decisive was how each one reacted to the great promise.

So it is with us. The response of each one to the spectacular promise given in Jesus makes our lives either meaningful or senseless. The Eucharist offers a decisive choice between intimacy with God or meaninglessness. There is no middle ground. We are helped up from the ditch to be robed for the wedding banquet or to be cast into outer darkness. There is no staying in the ditch anymore.

God bends over to embrace us and to pour into us the new wine of divine life. All we are asked to do is open our mouths and be fed like infants (see Psalm 81:11). Thus does Jesus seed our imagination. Once he institutes the ritual, he relaxes: "I have many more things to say to you but you cannot bear it now" (John 16:12). All in good time.

Jesus' choice to move to ritual is much like the Father's choice to bring about the incarnation. The Eucharist is as apt an embodiment of God's desire to be intimate with us as God could devise. "Whosoever eats me will live because of me" (John 6:57).

We are often reluctant to imagine intimacy with God. From childhood we learn that we are not the center of the universe. We learn this lesson with difficulty, and once we have learned it we are reluctant to let it go. Then an image is offered to us that says: "You are the center of the universe because God loves you as his other self."

Jesus' appreciation of the central role of the imagination in human life enabled him to move easily into the world of ritual. He knew we must enter the realm of imagination, myth, and story to be saved.

When I enter into the story of Jesus effectively made present through the Eucharist, I eat the flesh and blood of Jesus, the very substance of God. If I go through life with all its daily banalities, commuting between home and work, paying the bills, providing for the children's education, shopping, and all the while believing that I eat God's body and blood, then I am in another story. We think our life is this, that, or the other thing. But the Eucharist sweeps us up into another world; the Eucharist with its ritualistic repetition insists that our life is actually a meal that is happening in a totally different story. "All of life is a holy banquet."

Joachim Jeremias' words take on a rich meaning when they are applied to the Eucharist: "The inclusion of sinners in the community of salvation, achieved in table-fellowship, is the most meaningful expression of the message of the redeeming love of God."[9]

Every secular meal we eat confronts us with the charity we must show to our brothers and sisters at table and thereby prepares us for the Eucharist. The Eucharist is the beginning of the heavenly banquet because of the real presence of the Risen One. It is the way we await him "till he comes back again" for good (1 Cor 11:26).

"God *so* loved the world that he gave his only begotten Son." The Eucharist is the central symbol of the fulfillment of God's once-secret decision. The secret is fully revealed only in the Eucharist, and the secret is that God has chosen to offer us unlimited intimacy with him. It is the strongest symbol we have of being assumed into another story.

Because of Jesus, God is as preoccupied with our resurrection as with the resurrection of Jesus. God wants us to be equally preoccupied with our coming resurrection. The image of resurrection and the anticipatory joy of resurrection can enliven everything in our dull, anxious lives and fill us with peace and hope. New energy is coming to us out of the future. We say in the prayer that follows the Our Father: "Deliver us from all anxiety *as we wait in joyful hope* for the coming of our Savior, Jesus Christ." That anticipatory joy delivers us in the present from all anxiety.

In Albert Camus' *The Stranger,* a prisoner who has been sentenced to death reflects about his view of life:

> Nothing, nothing had the least importance, and I knew quite well why. [The chaplain] too, knew why. From the dark horizon of my future a sort of slow, persistent breeze had been blowing toward me, all my life long, from the years that were to come. And on its way that breeze had leveled out all the ideas that people tried to foist on me in the equally unreal years I was living through.... What did it matter...? As a condemned man himself, couldn't he grasp what I meant by that dark wind blowing from my future?[10]

Each of us is under the same sentence of death. What can it matter whether a life is lived this way or that when every life eventually fades into nothingness? God wants to deliver us from the deadly breeze that blows toward us, the call of illusion. God wants us refreshed in the midst of our guilt, despair, anxiety, and lovelessness. He wants us to taste now the future prepared for us. We are to spend our days like the ditch dweller on the way to the banquet hall and like the peasants awaiting the arrival of the tsar's treasury officials. God invites us to live like Charles at boarding school after his mother promises to come and get him after all, never forgetting the glory we draw closer to each day. God has placed words in our ears that invite us to imagine ourselves being raised from death. God's story has crossed our own, and that must be the center of our spiritual life.

In the Eucharist, we open our mouths. God fills us with divine life through the agonizing death of Jesus. Our sickness is so great that it leads to God's death and can only be healed by God's life. The Eucharist assures us that what we need is being given to us, freely and without cost. It invites us to live in the certitude of God's love for each of us. No matter what appears to be happening, the truth about our world's reality is that we are the arena where God's kindly will is working our salvation.

> "So it is," said Malle,
> "that already, little as they may know it,
> He hath all men taken in His net.
> And when He will, He may hale in, to bring us all home.
> How else? Shall that Strong One fail of His purpose?
> Or that Wise, who made all, be mistook?"[11]

Chapter Six

Spirituality for the Eucharist

In the first chapter, we spelled out how easy it is to talk and write of spirituality without mentioning the Eucharist, and to write about liturgy without mentioning gospel spirituality. In searching for the missing link we now raise the question: Is there a spirituality that needs the Eucharist as its vital center? Is Eucharist's deepest meaning such that it cannot be spoken of except in the context of Christian spirituality?

There is a parallel problem that might help us to see the cause of this split between liturgy and spirituality: it concerns the notion of grace in Christian theology. In 1948 Thomas Torrance wrote a book entitled *The Doctrine of Grace in the Apostolic Fathers.*[1] His purpose was to "probe into the early Christian understanding of grace, and to discern how and why there came about in the history of that doctrine so great a divergence from the teaching of the New Testament."[2] Karl Barth had suggested the study to Torrance, and Oscar Cullmann offered him many helpful suggestions. It was not difficult for Torrance to find one text after another in which early writers demonstrate their misunderstanding of the nature of grace. This continued for centuries and "some of the implications of the Gospel, grace particularly, were never recovered till the Reformation."[3]

In *Stromata* 7 and 8, Clement of Alexandria illustrates Torrance's point when he says: "He who holds converse with God must have his soul immaculate and stainlessly pure." That eliminates those most in need from holding converse with God. A similar passage is: "Wherefore those who are unworthy, though they ask often, he will not give; but he will give to those who are worthy." These are typical of the many texts that contradict the reality that grace is freely given, a gift.

However, this problem was not just with the apostolic fathers nor did it last just until the Reformation. It is still present today. Modern writers use the phrase "unearned gifts," and caution people not to ask for them in prayer. We must only ask for earned gifts—but that's salary talk, not gift talk. It is the same age-old infection at work, constantly reducing the incredible gift nature of grace. One writer admits that "becoming a friend of God cannot be earned, but it can be won as a prize."[4] But we don't have to win a gift. Reducing the notion of grace and emptying it of its incredible meaning is an ongoing error.

The apostolic fathers did not start this misunderstanding. It goes all the way back to the apostles themselves. They continually resisted acknowledging their lack of faith despite Jesus' persistent efforts to get them to be honest about it. This is a deep flaw in human nature: we avoid problems we cannot solve. We live in darkness because we are reluctant to look beyond the areas of our competence. We see every situation as a challenge to get to work. We already know why we are here on Earth: to receive the rewards due to our efforts. The following aphorisms express this concept well:

> Effort is its own reward.
> We are here to do,
> And through doing to learn;…
> and through attention
> to see what needs to be done.[5]

We see it as our job, and we groan. St. Augustine laments that we do not believe in Jesus' assurance that his yoke is sweet and his burden light; even believers consider the yoke of the devil more bearable. He writes of useless faith that believes in dogmas, but does not believe that the task is God's, not ours.[6] That is how the good news of God's gifts becomes the more believable "bad news" of the difficult but doable task that confronts us.

The recurring misunderstanding of the nature of grace springs from a flaw in the depths of the human condition. The separation of the liturgy and spirituality arises from that same deep flaw, a flaw that twists their roles and puts them on separate paths.

In their origins, these two areas of gospel life were united. What meaning did Jesus find that bound them together? Are there patterns in the Gospels that reveal a specific type of spiritual direction? In order to solve the problem, it is essential to uncover Jesus' own spirituality. What, then, was his spirituality? How did it incorporate Eucharist in its very essence?

Jesus left the apostles with a ritual. He gave the simple instruction: "Do it!" There is no indication that the early disciples theorized about that ritual, but they did indeed do it. They did it, and the impact on the early church was enormous. By entering the ritual they were letting God reveal to them who Jesus was. Their understanding of his true dignity developed rapidly. What did they bring to the early Eucharist that enabled it to have such an impact? What made it work so well? Jesus had led them along a path of spiritual direction that demanded this ritual.

One of the keys to Jesus' approach was his emphasis on the imagination. He spoke in parables. A king invites everyone to a wedding banquet for his son. That is the context of life on Earth, what we are here for: to receive an invitation to a splendid banquet.

Jesus offers no proof. He asserts. He wants to make his hearers wonder: "Is this what life is all about?" To be alive is to be present at a spectacular giveaway. That is why God brought us into this world out of nothingness. Jesus is suggesting that our lives could be so different, filled with joyful anticipation for the great banquet in heaven. As Karl Rahner put it:

> God wishes to communicate himself, to pour forth the love which he himself is. That is the first and last of his real plans and hence of his real world, too. Everything else exists so that this one thing might be: the eternal miracle of infinite love. And so God makes a creature whom he can love: he creates him. He creates him in such a way that we can receive this love which is God himself, and that he can and must at the same time accept it for what it is: the ever astounding wonder, the unexpected, the unexacted gift.[7]

In a way, Jesus is like a salesman. He makes spectacular promises about the splendor of what he has in his sample case. A new age is coming in, the true kingdom of God. Like every salesman, Jesus says:

"Believe me!" This first step makes up a large slice of Jesus' preaching. But Jesus encounters a persistent lack of faith, even in the apostles.

Promises are ineffective unless the hearer believes, and Jesus knew his listeners did not believe. A problem has arisen. How does he deal with it? It's especially difficult because the apostles are convinced that they *do* believe.

There is an event Luke recorded that can help us see how Jesus saw the path he must follow to accomplish his mission. The disciples have been sent on a mission and they return overjoyed with the success they have had. Striking signs accompanied their preaching, and they are delighted as they share their experiences with each other. They are like the winning team talking in the locker room after the championship game. Notice what Jesus does. He downplays all the signs. "Do not rejoice in this!" Forget the signs. They are not important.

This is very much what he did in his own mission. He refused to call people's attention to his miracles. He downplayed them. Signs are visible: he focused attention on faith instead. Faith is a way of relating to the invisible, of knowing something even without proofs. If you have faith, you do not need proofs; you do not even look for them.

Jesus does the same with his rejoicing disciples. He invites them to focus on something invisible: the Father's great love for them: "Rejoice that your names are written in heaven" (Luke 10:20). This heavenly writing is not visible. It cannot be seen or proven. But it can be imagined. Jesus has led the disciples away from what they can see to what they can only imagine: God sitting on his throne writing *their* names down in a book.

Jesus doesn't prove it. He asserts it. He invites the disciples to imagine it. The imagination is the faculty of the infinite. Jesus wants them to rise up from the world of appearances to the real. "What if the Creator of heaven and earth has written your name in his book? Imagine!"

This was typical of Jesus' preaching. He did not prove. He asserted the good news and invited people to let it become alive in their imagination. The good news would appeal because of its goodness. It was too good not to be true. It is as if God and his kingdom work like a shepherd who cannot sleep until he finds the lost sheep and brings it home on his shoulders.

Wouldn't that be splendid, if only it were true? Jesus projects this spectacular possibility into their imaginations. That's how he planted the seed. True joy would come only to those who believed in this spectacular but unproved possibility.

The joy the disciples experienced in rehearsing their successes was certain to be taken away when the signs failed. The day was coming when there would be no signs. But the joy Jesus wanted them to have was to be permanent, a joy no one could take from them. That could come only to those who welcomed into their imaginations this incredible scenario and chose to believe it. He was offering them a permanent source of joy. Whether there were signs or no signs at all, still there was the truth: God has written your name in his book.

There are many other instances of Jesus' calling the apostles' attention to their lack of real faith. One occurs when Jesus and the apostles are on a lake during a storm. After trying their best to save the boat, these fishermen go to the back of the boat, wake up the carpenter, and ask him to save them. That looks like faith in Jesus, doesn't it? But when they wake him up and he miraculously calms the storm, he reproaches them for their *lack* of faith.

What is he getting at? Like a good spiritual director, Jesus is helping them to get at least a brief glimpse of the life of real faith. To do it he gets them to take notice of their feelings: "You of little faith, why were you terrified?" (Matt 8:26).

On another occasion, he reproaches Peter. Jesus was walking on the water. At the Lord's invitation, Peter stepped out of the boat onto the water. Wasn't that faith? When the waves began to frighten him he began to sink, and he called to Jesus. Jesus helped him but said: "Why did you doubt, O you of little faith?" (Matt 14:31). Jesus gets Peter to look at his emotion. He raises the apostles' and Peter's sights to a way of life that is impossible to believe, free of all anxiety in the knowledge of God's loving power, no matter how bleak things appear.

Jesus capitalized on such moments. When Martha chided Jesus for letting Mary get away with not helping, Jesus urged Martha to look at what was happening within her: "You are worried about so many things" (Luke 10:41).

The apostles in the boat, Peter on the waves, and Martha, all could have said: "Of course we are anxious. What alternative is there?" What alternative way of being present in such situations does Jesus propose? Believing with a faith that needs no signs at all. The day is coming when God, despite his omnipotence, is going to be crucified, and sign-faith will be useless.

When the apostles could not cure a possessed boy, Jesus spelled it out again: "Had you even faith the size of a mustard seed, you could move mountains." But they cannot move mountains. Their faith is smaller than a single speck of pepper. If they were to hold up their faith between their thumb and their index finger, no one would be able to see it. Much of Jesus' energy goes into getting his disciples to see that their faith is shallow. Unless faith deepens, the promises of a splendid way of living will have no impact.

In addition to preaching this new way of believing, Jesus also raises their sights to a higher way of life in the area of loving. When Jesus speaks to Martha of her anxiety, he mentions this: "There is need of only one thing" (Luke 10:42). For Jesus that one thing is specified in the Love Command.

When it comes to the kind of loving he insists on, Jesus again uses the imagination. When Peter asks how often he must forgive (Matt 18:21 ff.), Jesus uses a parable to help him glimpse a different way of forgiving, forgiving from the heart. It's the parable about a man who refuses to forgive an injustice and how this refusal shocks his fellow servants.

Jesus pictures that first servant, caught in a catastrophe, a debt so big that he cannot pay. He will be sold, together with his wife, his children, and all he owns. But his master forgives him freely. Jesus is inviting Peter to picture a person like the first servant, forgiven an enormous debt, who would therefore feel obliged to forgive another. He would go out looking for opportunities to free those in need of his forgiveness, as he had been forgiven. His heart would go out to them as he remembered his own agony and how he was delivered. Being obliged to forgive would be a sweet yoke, a light burden.

"What if, Peter, you knew yourself to have committed an unspeakable betrayal of someone who loved and trusted you?" Jesus is trying to get Peter to enter the heart of someone in great need of being forgiven. If he can only get him to taste what it *would* be like to be forgiven for something unforgivable, Peter will have a chance to glimpse this new kind of loving.

Jesus used images on another occasion when he was trying to lead one of the Pharisees to see this new path. He told of someone who owed a moneylender more money than he could earn in a year. A second debtor owed the moneylender a much smaller amount. The moneylender cancels both debts. Jesus then asked Simon the Pharisee, "Now which of them will love him more?" (Luke 7:36 ff.).

Simon found that easy. "The one who owed the greater sum." Jesus underlines it: "The one to whom little is forgiven, loves little." It is a strange new world. In order to love as Jesus demands, you must be forgiven much. Sinners have the edge.

But when Peter heard the invitation to see himself as a traitor, he could not accept it. It was beyond imagining that he would ever betray a friend. He could not imagine the life of freely forgiving from the heart that would follow the joy of being forgiven.

What is this new way of relating to people who injure us? A path of persistent forgiving. How can God oblige us to forgive endlessly? Because he forgives us for the much greater debt that we owe. Who is willing to enter into such an unpleasant image of themselves? "Other people may do that but I will never betray a friend, Lord." In these incidents, Jesus tries to persuade Peter and Simon the Pharisee to enter this new kingdom. It will take imagination and self-honesty.

On many occasions Jesus responds to the competitiveness of his disciples, their jealousies, their wrestling for the top spot. He even compares their behavior to that of the worst pagans, who lord it over each other whenever they have the power. "It must not be so among you," he says (Matt 20:26). Like a good salesman, he uses eloquence to describe this new world. He is hoping they will wonder: "What if this is true?"

Obviously this approach is appropriate for beginners, but what is Jesus' way of directing those on the higher levels of the spiritual life? Surprisingly, there is no other way. All of us, no matter what level we are at, constantly need to have our imaginations seeded anew with images of where we could be.

What does Jesus hope will happen? That his listeners will hear his words and give their imagination to his seeding. If that happens, they will be filled with the desire to enter into that kingdom, to live each day with deeper faith in God and love for others like Jesus' own love for them.

When a salesman succeeds, his audience is dissatisfied with their life. They have glimpsed a better life, and it could be theirs for $9.99 plus tax. They act. They buy the product. So, too, Jesus was trying to produce dissatisfaction in his audience, to get them to act. What is it that he wants them to do in their desire and dissatisfaction? To try their best to be that trusting, that loving? No. He had another way: "Ask and you shall receive." They will not enter this new world unless they become like children, asking for what they want even if they cannot pay for it. That was news indeed: "It's yours for the asking." His disciples were to become people constantly turning to God and asking for the gifts of faith and love.

Another pattern in Jesus' spiritual direction was urging people to ask persistently. One author calls it "the fundamental spiritual attitude of the disciple."[8] He is commenting on Luke 17:5, the only place in the Gospels where the apostles ask for faith. Why don't they persist? Because they were convinced that they already had faith. They couldn't imagine themselves as people of little faith. They felt no need for deeper faith.

Did Jesus see much success in his way of directing his disciples? What fired their desire was the promise of the twelve thrones on which they would soon be sitting, not the life of faith and love. Jesus hoped to give them a faith that needed no signs at all. That would bring them up Calvary's hill. But it did not happen. After the passion the apostles at last were able to feel like unforgivable traitors, and all of Jesus' words about their lack of faith and their need to ask came back to haunt them.

While he was with them, they blurred his very clear commands. After the passion they could see that he had been following a straight path all along, never giving up. It was clear to them now. They told others the sad tale of their blindness, and in time that tale became our good news. They were born anew in their cowardice by God's freely forgiving them. In forgiving others, their sins made sense.

The Gospels portray the spirituality of Jesus at great length. He did not focus on methods or quantity of prayer. Instead he repeatedly emphasized the crucial role that honesty plays. Parables on humility urge us to bring our sinfulness to the surface when we go to pray. "Take the lowest place at the table" (Luke 14:9–10) was not a suggestion on how to win the esteem of people but how to present yourself before God. Effective prayer was honest prayer—"Lord, have mercy on me, a sinner" (Luke 18:13)—the prayer of those aware of their need. Their very need for God would guarantee their closeness to him.

This was Jesus' way of directing his disciples, his spirituality. He revealed the splendid life that God had created them for, a life lived off the power of the Spirit. He helped them see how far they were from being there. He urged them to ask for it persistently.

The Last Supper had little impact on the disciples. It was not that Jesus failed to explain it to them. No, the Eucharist had no impact on the Twelve because they refused to be present to it. There were twelve frightened men at that table, and Jesus wanted to talk to them and heal them. But they brought their fears in the door as they entered the Upper Room. There was nobody for Jesus to talk to; he was already alone. His words fell on deaf ears. They did not need this ritual in which anxiety could be removed by a deeper gift of faith. They were already willing to die for him—at least, so they believed. After Calvary they were humiliated. Their awareness of the dishonesty they lived in dominated those early days. The ritual act was for those lacking faith and love.

Christian spirituality must keep returning to the Gospels, to watch Jesus at work in order to be authentic. That return will reveal the intimate link Jesus saw existing between his great ritual act and his spirituality.

Today God acts on us and within us exactly as Jesus did with his disciples. We do not hear Jesus' voice, but the reading of scripture can play a vital role in our spiritual life. In reading we encounter images of a God who wants to raise us to new levels of existence, to clothe us with garments of faith and love, even to clothe us with Jesus himself. Our highest potential, far more filled with joy, more trusting of God, more assured of God's love, more sensitive to the needs of others—that is what God has in mind when gazing at us.

We are like the disciples. We begin our spiritual life with much confidence. We already know that life is a struggle to ascend a mountain. To be near God we must make sacrifices; in fact, we must sacrifice our most precious possession. We feel we know the meaning of love, faith, grace, and prayer. If we are to enter into the true meaning, we have to be stripped of our present knowledge. We have to become ignorant, but with an ignorance that isn't there in the beginning, ignorance we must learn. By giving us glimpses of the true nature of grace and the Eucharist, God helps us to realize how deceived we are. By these moments of truth he brings to birth someone who is eager for the gift of genuine love (1 Pet 1:22–23).

God must get *us* to imagine what we could be, to glimpse the greater life he invites us to receive. God uses sacred scripture to seed our imagination with images of what our lives could be like. *We* could now be experiencing inexhaustible joy. *We* could be the abode of God. *We* could be exalted in prayer. *We* could be aware of God's trustworthiness as Jesus was. Long ago God decided to make us more like Jesus. What would happen if we began to believe that?

Through the reading and study of scripture, God plants the seed in our hearts. This planting continues until our death, and from this planting, our spiritual life grows. God deliberately points us in the direction of the splendor that could be.

In his *Spiritual Exercises,* Ignatius of Loyola suggests that at the beginning of each prayer we consider how God is gazing at us. How *does* God gaze at us? What kind of a look is on God's face? Is it like a mother's as she watches her baby daughter crawl on the floor and at the same time sees her walking upright, even though that is still to come? Even though the little girl has no idea that this will happen, nonetheless, in her mother's imagination, she is walking. The mother desires it, has an agenda for her child. She is determined her child will walk. This is a part of her motherly love.

Strangely, we resist this image of the self and prefer not to imagine it. It is a future we must make ourselves worthy of. The more splendid it is, the greater the price we must pay. And so we qualify the promises of God until they mean just a little more than the status quo. We substitute a smaller, more realistic, more attainable future in place of what the gospel offers. We are careful not to get too excited about future possibilities. We discount what God has promised. That is for the saints, not for us.

This kind of false humility enables us to satisfy God by working at being just a little better than we are. "If I just try a little harder, I'm sure God will be pleased." Now we have a task we *can* do. Unfortunately, we have silenced God's voice. We no longer hear him tell us of that faith-filled person he wants us to become. The dialogue with God is over.

How do we get around this detour? We must be honest. We must use our imagination to glimpse a God who means it. "What if God means what he says?" Our decision to hear God's incredible promises is essential to our spiritual growth. To our willingness to be honest, Jesus attaches an experience of such intensity that he calls it *exaltation* (Matt 23:12). Experiencing such exaltation comes only to the humble, the honest.

The ability to pray honestly from the heart also requires knowledge of our behavior in the concrete choices of each day. We have to see ourselves refusing affection to this one, judging that one, and being indifferent toward another. Without such specific knowledge of our unloving behavior, our confession of sinfulness is only on our lips. It is an admission we know we should make, and one we may think we are making sincerely. We must choose to look at ourselves turning away from love if we want to pray effectively. Without this examination we do not see what God never loses sight of: how much of us is yet unredeemed.

In 1 Samuel 18, Jonathan sees his dear friend David as he is, dressed shabbily. But he also sees a David that could be, dressed like the royal Jonathan himself. Jonathan shares his own clothing with David—robe, armor, sword, bow, belt. He takes David as his other self.

This is an image of one who loves. What if God is seeking, during our lifetime, for ways to clothe us in his heavenly garments? What if that is the fundamental meaning of life? If we really believed that, our experience of day-to-day life would be so different. We would live filled with the anticipatory joy that the Eucharist speaks of. The promises would fill us with consuming desire.

Praying without any sense of what God desires to bring about dilutes its power. If we are unaware of any greater breadth of loving or believing than we already have, we will remain unmoved before God's offer. But if we are aware of how far we are from the joy of full faith, we will desire, and with that desire will come dissatisfaction with the present state of our spirit. After *hearing the promises* and *desiring* what they offer, this *dissatisfaction* with where we are spiritually is the third basic element of gospel spirituality.

While it is normal to fear getting into an area that can be depressing, the *gospel* calls us to trust that we can, in Jesus' power, afford to be honest about ourselves, endlessly honest. We are called to trust that as we see what hypocrites we are in our readiness to deal justice to others and mercy to ourselves, our despair will not be unto death. To share the Lord's hopes for us, to experience him willing it so boldly despite the cost he knows he must pay, and to see where we are and the unlikelihood that we will ever be able to fulfill the Law will produce constant despair. This *despair* is the fourth element that is present in the spiritual direction Jesus gives to his followers. Repeated experiences of despair have an important role in the spiritual life: despair frees us from trying to build our spiritual life on our own terms. For the first disciples this came only on the day they stayed away from Calvary.

God invites us to walk in the desert of our spiritual poverty. Like the man in the land of the Gerasenes (Mark 5:1–20), we will see ourselves as the great enemy of our own happiness. We become the sinners who cause Jesus' death, who need his death to deliver us, and who hear him assure us: "It is, indeed, for you that this blood is poured out. Open your mouth and I will fill it with divine life."

St. Thomas Aquinas says that the motive for prayer is the desire for the gift of love.[9] Instead of a mountain we must scale, the saints talk of an elevator we must look for. Instead of a ladder that we must climb, Karl Adam spoke of our beginning at the top rung. Instead of sowing and reaping, we are invited to look at the ravens who do neither, but feed freely from the Father's hands.

The demands of the Law will not be put aside; not an iota of the Law will be changed. It will be fulfilled to the letter, but in a manner no one had ever dreamed of. Incredibly, we will fulfill the Law because we will inherit that fulfillment. An unexpected inheritance will totally change our lives. Faith in that inheritance will free us to look at our past honestly. Past sin will lose its power to alienate us from God. The joy of being forgiven will fuel a new way of living. It will act as an energy source permitting us to look fearlessly at our weakness.

There is a paradox connected with loving that may help in recognizing the importance of choosing to see our lack of love: love is not self-conscious. If one is conscious of loving, the love is not deep. As love deepens, our eyes look only at the other. It is like the man who was driving home in an ice storm in Washington, worried about whether he had enough gas. Suddenly, he was leaping from his car into the icy river, rescuing a drowning victim of a plane crash. When he reached shore, reporters were eager to talk with him; people wanted to make much of his heroic deed.

He found it all quite strange. Why such a fuss? He felt he had done what anybody would in such a situation. He didn't notice dozens of people standing along the bank. His consciousness was filled with what he saw, a person drowning. There was no room there for him to see the heroism of his response.

As love comes into our lives, it brings a deepening awareness of the needs of others and an accompanying realization of how much greater our response could be. The Spirit's coming enlarges our hearts to perceive needs we formerly had not allowed ourselves to see. What if we had been standing on the shore with all the others, hoping the rescuers would arrive in time? Then we get a momentary glimpse of the victim's face and realize it is our mother. A surge of energy would come into us then. What if we saw it was Jesus? Love would open our eyes to feel the danger as if it were happening to us.

If we pass a ragged man sitting on the sidewalk with his hat upside down in front of him, we may feel good about ourselves when we drop in five dollars. But what if there is also blood streaming from his mouth, which we ignored because to see it would interrupt our schedule? Once we let ourselves see that blood, we will lose all sense of how loving our action is. When we open our eyes to the truth about the terrible needs around us, the Spirit makes us shiver at our indifference and at our impulsive reluctance to respond. To get to know love is to become ever more aware of unlove. Hans Urs von Balthasar puts it this way in *Love Alone:* "As we get to know what true love is, we become aware at the same time, and unanswerably, that we have no true love."[10]

In saving us, God does not point to triumphs in our inner life. God's success is secret, known only to faith. The divine gifts are not seen even after they are received. The path is dark.

> Lord God, you have called your servants to ventures of which we cannot see the ending, by paths yet untrod, through perils unknown. Give us faith to go out with good courage, not knowing where we go, but only that your hand is leading and your love supporting us.[11]

My horizon fills up with my weakness. In that void God's will to save me and my brothers and sisters becomes my only consolation. But it is an abundant, never-failing consolation.

Just as Jesus tried to fill the disciples' imagination with images of their glorious inheritance, today God wants us to imagine that splendor.

Just as Jesus capitalized on moments when he could help the disciples to uncover their unlove, their competitiveness, their pattern of ignoring the needs of others, so, today, God wants us to imagine vividly those decisions springing from our unlove.

That person whom we feel we can live without, for whom we feel no affection and not the least desire for affection, that person is loved by God intensely. It is in facing the enemy that we see who we are and who God is. We fear to love. We are set to defend our rights. To use covenant language, God is *hesed,* a heart filled with compassion for our enemies, endlessly affectionate and forgiving, refusing to give up or turn his back on any of us.

Are we willing to imagine a God who has great affection for our enemies? Jesus led his hearers to form that image in his parable of the prodigal son. Imagining such a God is vital. It is an essential step in getting to know God, in letting him reveal his true face to us. Otherwise, we, like the elder brother, will be shocked and repelled when we finally do encounter the strange face of the true God.

God wants to refashion us along these lines. At times it sounds like an invitation to let ourselves be crucified. When they saw themselves locked in blind unloving even the saints were repelled. *Loathsome* was a common description for what they saw within their own hearts. A part of them was in the power of a demon bent on destruction, and was anti-gospel in its convictions.

Besides the face of the enemy, we must let the face of the poor enter our consciousness. We would rather "do something" for the poor than look into their faces. But it is only *looking* that leads to effective action. We need to expose ourselves to their lives deliberately. We need to look carefully at the way the poor live. But the face of the poor is not easily available to us. Our society has gone to great lengths to protect us from that sight.

What would happen if we noticed the poor each day? We would feel guilty, and this helps explain our reluctance. A close look at poverty brings on an awareness of all we fail to do. In these emotions, we may see ourselves terrified at the thought of getting involved. This is such a contrast with the Lord, who can never avert his eyes from the poor. A loving choice keeps him fixed in a sleepless gaze, filled with determination to help them.

The face of the poor reveals the Lord to us, his own face filled with horror at the pain we inflict on each other. Do we really want to be united with such a God? God has very peculiar preferences. One may pretend to be interested in classical music if one's beloved is a Mozart fan. One may try to learn chess to share that part of the beloved's life. Are we eager to be with Jesus as he gazes at the face of the poor?

Do we try to imagine union with God in a way that ignores who God really is? This is our inclination. We unite with a domesticated god, created in our own image, a god who never reminds us of our lack of love and with whom we can spend hours without ever a thought about the lot of the poor. Such a god is not the God of the Bible, whose concern for the poor and the oppressed is unwavering. God has an intense desire to share that concern with us. To be in the presence of God is to experience a blazing concern.

These two faces must be the substance of our self-examination: the faces of the poor and of our "enemies" will lead us to the truth about ourselves. This truth leads to effective participation in the Eucharist and to being touched most fully by God's salvific actions. God cannot force us to receive his offer of joy as he forces us to receive the gift of life. God's agenda is to get us to accept the gift of joy. How does he go about it? In one of her visions, Julian of Norwich heard the Lord talk about the steps:

> Our Lord said: I am the ground of your beseeching. First, it is my will that you should have it, and then I make you to wish it, and then I make you to beseech it....

He then told her of his joy when he encounters our willingness to receive:

> How could you please me more than by entreating me, urgently, wisely, and sincerely, to do the thing that I want to have done?[12]

God wants us to experience his own great joy. But God's joy flows from his love. He must get us to receive the gift of loving as he does. He commands us to love like that, and he isolates that command as the one thing necessary. We must put on the wedding garment (Matt 22:11), or as Paul puts it, the armor of God (Eph 6:13). We must put on

the Lord Jesus Christ (Rom 13:14). That is nothing but the gift of loving as God loves.

But the hearing of God's promises is not an early stage of spiritual
growth that we leave behind as we approach sanctity. The desire and
dissatisfaction that spring from believing in the divine promises are not
just for beginners. As we approach God, we grow in desire for what
God holds out to us, and we become increasingly dissatisfied with
where we are. St. Teresa of Avila insisted that getting to know the true
self would always be necessary, even in the highest mansions. The need
to be honest can never be ignored.

In the Church of St. Ignatius in Rome, the entire ceiling is an opti-
cal illusion. In the center of the floor there is a circular copper disk. If
you stand right on it, you can look up and see the walls of the church
rising far above to an open sky filled with angels and saints. But once
you move off the copper disk, everything is out of focus. You can still
tell what the artist intended, but you do not experience the illusion.

There is such a copper disk in Christianity. When we stand on it,
we experience the power of the Gospels and are drawn into a new way
of perceiving our existence. As we grow in the freedom to look at ourselves honestly, we will experience the intense dissatisfaction that is
the copper disk of gospel spirituality. We groan as we see the petty,
self-serving ways in which we spend our days and the fear-filled paths
along which we walk.

Long before he introduced his apostles to his ritual, Jesus spent
endless energy trying to bring them into the real world. The Eucharist
cannot have any impact on those who live in illusion. He used every
opportunity to help them see that their faith was shallow. He tried to
humble them so that they would experience the exaltation prepared for
them in the eucharistic ritual. "Learn from me," he said, but he was not
speaking of the gifts of faith and love, for they are not learned but
implanted. Humility, honesty, being real—these can be learned, and
Jesus taught them.

But he failed. The apostles clung to their illusions right through
the first Eucharist. They were present at the great mystery of grace, but
they were possessed by an image of themselves as real believers,
heroes who would die with their Lord. Their refusal to see themselves
honestly left them unaware of how much they needed the gift the

Eucharist offered. Their weak faith was not enough to keep them close to Jesus in his great moment of need. They let him go his way alone.

But life taught them the lesson they needed. Their cowardice quickly became clear to them. Calvary opened their eyes. Now they knew what Jesus meant by "worthless servants." When he came to them in his risen body and ate with them, they became aware of their need to be forgiven the unforgivable; they experienced Jesus' desire to forgive even that.

At the Last Supper they had not been amazed at being invited. It seemed appropriate for them to be there. They belonged. But at the Easter Eucharists they would appreciate Jesus' praise of the centurion's words: "Lord, I am not worthy that you should come under my roof." Peter may have relived the experience that began his life with Jesus and the words he said then: "Leave me, Lord, for I am a sinful man" (Luke 5:8). Just as he had exalted Peter then by calling him to join him, so the risen Jesus now calls their humbled hearts to preach to the whole world (Mark 16:14–15).

Those who are aware of their need for the power to believe, for the power to love, experience the eucharistic event as the one thing necessary. It becomes the constant distraction of their day, which, while it must be turned away from so that they can work, fills them with joy even as it leaves. Just as those with an honest image of their weakness understand the notion of grace, so too, they become preoccupied with the coming eucharistic encounter with the Lord.

Who can hear with joy the message of good news that Jesus embodied in the Eucharist: "I can forgive your past, and I do; I can heal your weakness, and I do; I assure you of your future"? Only those who are facing their guilt, their inability to love, their anxiety, their dread of death.

When we feel a desperate need for God to step in and act, we find the Eucharist meaningful. "Hope in God begins at the very moment when we despair of ourselves."[13] That was the paschal experience of the apostles. "Not only can the soul which recognizes its poverty have great confidence in God, but it can only have true confidence if it does recognize it."[14] Those who are in touch with their guilt, anxiety, and lack of love are so in need of hearing the message in the core ritual that

they hear it even when the sermon is not helpful. They hear it as something too good to be true, too splendid not to be true.

Jesus was aware that until we see what we are up against, we are
tilting at windmills. What we are up against is more than human, and
our weapons are water pistols. Our struggle is "against the sovereign-
ties and the powers who originate the darkness in this world, the spiritual army of evil in the heavens" (Eph 6:12). We must "call in the
marines." That is what prayer is, a distress call: asking "God and Jesus
Christ, who is our sole liberator, that he save us, because we feel in ourselves such great moments of infirmity that, if he did not sustain us at
every moment by new graces, we would perish."[15]

Are we in such peril? We may not think so, but such is the experience of the saints from the earliest times who constantly searched for
the true self. "The Early Fathers considered knowing oneself as a
whole scheme of Christian life, not one activity of many as the examen.
It is as though examen were made into a way of Christian life."[16] We
need to discover powerlessness within us. That is what Jesus sought to
produce in the apostles.

Being honest means seeing how undeserving we are. This can have
the unfortunate effect of lowering our expectations in prayer. Ordinarily
if we think we have been generous and tried to progress in our spiritual
life, we expect a response. If we feel we have not been serious, we will go
to prayer with little expectation that the Lord will come. But the gospel
gifts are available only to those who *do* see their constant failures clearly
but *still* expect the Lord to come to them. When Jesus sought for an
image of the ideal pray-er he used that of the child, "the finest example of
the poor man, a being defenseless and powerless who would not know
how to get by without the help of his parents."[17]

"For we don't know how to pray as we ought" (Rom 8:26 *NRSV*).
"It is very important for us to realize that we do not know how to pray.
If we think of prayer as something we can master, we are in danger of
falsifying our relationship with God. This elusiveness of prayer, this
systematic impossibility of knowing how to do it, is an integral part of
the scriptural view of prayer."[18] We must enter into our incompetence
so that the Spirit may come as promised to help us in our weakness.

"When does the Word of God most often knock at your door?"
asks St. Ambrose.[19] "He visits in love those in trouble and temptation,

to save them from being overwhelmed by their trials." When you are experiencing weakness and distress, "that is the time you must keep watch....If your heart is watching, he knocks." St. Ignatius of Loyola insisted that even beginners should expect visitations of God, although their prayer is brief.[20]

The truth that we do not know how to pray is vital for an effective Eucharist. An English Carmelite writes of the union between liturgy and the deepest spirituality. When we stand before God in our poverty as a living need,

> [now] the sacraments come into their own. That which formerly could be received only partially, now meets with no obstacle. The utterly "alien" and "other," God himself, meets in the soul a life "other" to its depths. The sacramental encounter is continuous. Two abysses meet and know one another. Every reception of the sacraments means a deeper surrender and possession by God and always it is in the church and for the church.[21]

The little child looks to his mother with her spoonful of delicious food in her hand and responds to the invitation "Open your mouth." We too are invited: "Open your mouth and I will fill it" (see Psalm 81:11). Its fullness will fill our hearts as well. For Jesus the Eucharist was a specific response to specific needs: the disciples' unloving and their lack of faith. The gifts of faith and love produce a joyful life.

Just as Jesus led his disciples into dissatisfaction with their constant anxiety, the Spirit today prepares us for the eucharistic gifts. When we glimpse what we could be, we see what we *are* more clearly, with all our limitations. The fear that governs so many of our choices will stand out in contrast to the freedom we could have. The protective animosity in our relations with others will be illuminated by the concrete image of the more loving person that God has in mind. We must let God show us how thin our love for others is, and how thoroughly grounded in self-protection our instinctive reactions to people are. We will then come to the Eucharist in great need of its healing.

If we try to push down all our anger so that we can have a moment of peace when we go to the Eucharist or other prayer, we will not find God. We will be like a man with a broken toe who goes to a doctor's office to hear the music and read a magazine, to get a moment of peace.

He has lost touch with the will of the doctor, who did not open his office to provide moments of peace. Just as the doctor has a will that can go to work if you show him your broken toe, God needs you to be honest about your lack of love.

Just as the apostles had their Calvary experience, we encounter situations that force us to grow. When we are in pain, the image of God as a tender mother can seem unreal. We are in pain and God does not lift a finger to help us. We are tempted to resist God's intimacy. We try to ignore the invitation. An instinctive feeling may surface: "I'll put up with the pain, but don't tell me God loves me." We are not comfortable with the image of a God who runs to embrace us, when we know how much suffering God permits us to undergo. Our temptation is to ignore the problem and the negative, unprayerful feelings of abandonment.

This image of unlimited intimacy forces us to make a decision of faith at its deepest level. The confrontation with the problem of evil that must be faced in life demands absolute honesty. God invites us to dialogue about the pain. He invites us to express pain, anger, frustration, and feelings of injustice. Each Eucharist must begin with our entry into our true self. Efforts to produce an appropriate mood are self-defeating. Our wounded self must become present; the eucharistic rite is effective only when we encounter our real self face to face.

Great consolations are promised to people of faith who enter honestly into their negative feelings. We are invited to feel the destructive power of those negative emotions. Only the death and blood of God can be enough to heal these wounds. We must experience our despair at our inability to deal with them. We are promised strength and an assurance of God's love, consolation, and peace beyond imagining. We must experience how our emptiness leads to being filled, and how in our despair hope is born. In the faith experience God speaks and enables us to hear and believe with assurance despite his apparent abandonment of us.

In the Eucharist, Love meets unlove, and transforms it. The more fully I can acknowledge the unlove that I am, the more thoroughly God's power is active. As Thérèse of Lisieux remarks in a letter to Sister Marie of the Sacred Heart: "When he sees me without desire and without virtue, then he makes me the object of his consuming love."[22] We are most exalted when we are most aware of our alienation from God.

No exaggeration is needed, just honesty. There is no call to pretend to see evils we do not see. With the growing awareness of our patterns of concealment, we will find it realistic to presume that there are greater depths of selfishness yet uncovered. The gospel demands openness to the unloving choices we make now. There is no need to search out the past. The evil we do today is enough.

The gift we have to place on the altar is our emptiness. The old understanding of the "offertory" gave the impression that we were giving something to God, but all we can bring and all that God wants is our emptiness. It is said that St. Jerome once asked Jesus: "What more can I give you, Lord, that you do not already have?" The answer he received: "Give me your emptiness that I may fill it." We cannot give that to the Lord if we are unaware of it.

If we come to the Eucharist conscious of our day-to-day unlove, we will be eager for God's redemptive intervention. We will be ready to hear the Word of God spoken through the Eucharist. Christian spirituality is meant to help us enter fully into the liturgical reality, to make us thirsty for the living water of divine life that surges through the Eucharist. Our preparation for the Eucharist, our spirituality, must make us conscious of how much we need God to invade our life with new creative acts that surpass even the splendor of the original creation of the world.

We are saved if God is at work. If God is not at work, we can do nothing to fill the gap. We must stop wasting energy and hedging our bets in case our good behavior is demanded in the end. Rather, we must rest completely on God's desire to raise us up, which is known to us through faith alone. Even now God sees us glorified with Jesus' glory. God sees us in our risen bodies clothed with divine joy. This is his agenda. He calls on us to have that same agenda.

God brings to birth within us a child whose father he can be. God leads us to ask like a child. Our life thus comes to rest on two supports: the real world without illusions and the promises of God. If we wish to hear God in the Eucharist, and to receive his Spirit, we must first come face to face with our real selves.

How did Jesus prepare the disciples for the Last Supper, that first Eucharist? He didn't spend time explaining it. They didn't need to know. It was a gift, an action of God. They just had to be present. But to be present, they had to be in the real world—that was where it would happen. What did they have to bring? The knowledge of their need for God's action-gift. Jesus tried to produce just that. That was how he prepared the disciples for that first Eucharist.

How can people get this vital spiritual direction today? Having a personal director is more common today but still quite rare. Weekend retreats help. Studying the Gospels prayerfully is a path quite a few follow. But for most people being present at the Eucharist is the opportunity to be directed as Jesus directed his disciples.

The Gospel texts read at the Eucharist frequently offer us instances in which Jesus is giving spiritual direction. The homilist can help people hear Jesus promise a happy life to those who are humble or as he asks us to have a forgiving heart. One Sunday, Jesus is portrayed preaching a parable that helps people see their reluctance to accept his teaching. The next, Jesus promises that asking works if you are persistent. The next chapter will focus on that promise: "Ask and you shall receive."

Chapter Seven

Spirituality in the Eucharist

It is easier to apply the gospel to others than to ourselves. It is easy to see how other people should be honest about their imperfections, but getting us to be honest goes against our resistance to losing self-esteem. That's why we pay people to counsel us—we pay for their objective vision of what's happening within us. We count on them to open up our eyes to things we have hidden away and can no longer find.

Jesus offered that service to people freely. Preaching as Jesus did continues his mission of helping people see the dark resistance of their deepest reality. In the eucharistic rite, Jesus offers us a flow of healing power that enables us to relax into the truth of our inner self and its neediness. Jesus called people to live off the power of the new age. This gift is meant not to help us do our best, but to empower us to do far more than our best: to live as Jesus himself lived and loved, to tap the energies in the gifts of the Spirit.

The disciples did not need the Eucharist explained to them. They needed to be led into the real world; for those who live in the real world, the neediness is obvious. Preaching as Jesus did is not training people to doctor themselves but helping them to feel their spiritual wounds.

Jesus used parables to help people realize their reluctance to hear of a God who loves the wicked son despite his evil choices, who offers the same reward to the latecomers as to the early birds. He gave them a glimpse of what love is really like.

In the parable of the laborers in the vineyard, Jesus brought people to feel their resentment at what appears to be the owner's unfairness. Even today, people admit that they do not like this parable. We feel Jesus praises an injustice. It reveals to us the world we think we are in—a world of honest effort and its reward—and we lose sight of the gospel world. The listeners who feel they deserve a reward feel resentful. Those who feel they deserve little or nothing are greatly delighted.

The Gospels provide the preacher with many opportunities to preach as Jesus did. But there is another path for helping people be present at Eucharist effectively: teaching them to make the prayers of the Eucharist their own. Throughout the rite we offer prayers to God. Some express gratitude, others praise; many of them are prayers of petition. The presider prays in the name of all, but often the words are lost despite their truth and their beauty. In these prayers we find the spirituality of Jesus expressed in petitions to God. The very asking is an invitation to believe that all is ours for the asking, a central promise of Jesus' preaching.

We now turn to the eucharistic liturgy itself, in order to uncover the gospel spirituality expressed in its words and rites. The liturgy spells out fundamental Christian spirituality. It has been the prime vehicle for Christian formation throughout church history. It has played the role Jesus intended. The eucharistic texts and actions focus on our everyday world. They invite us to a more realistic vision of ourselves, and a more gospel vision of the Lord.

Imagine it is Friday, the third week of Advent. After the greeting and the penitential rite, the presider prays:

> All-powerful Father,
> guide us with your love
> as we await the coming of your Son.
> Keep us faithful
> that we may be helped through life
> and brought to *salvation*.

What does *salvation* mean? How does *salvation* become meaningful? What will change *salvation* from meaningless sounds to a word that expresses something important?

In order to become meaningful, these liturgical words must link to a reality deep within the worshiper. Suppose that worshiper is a woman who comes to the Eucharist before going to work. What if *salvation* only brings to mind an image of God rescuing the Israelites at the Red Sea? This is not inappropriate, but it is not enough. As she listens, she is not hostile to being brought to salvation, but neither do the words fire any yearning within. If asked, she could talk about it but without having a real stake in it. Being *brought to salvation* seems peripheral.

What are the realities within her that this phrase signals? Perhaps she is still angry about an unjust accusation made by her husband during a recent spat. Maybe *salvation* means the power to forgive unfairness without wanting to strike back. The urge to strike back can destroy our happiness for days.

At the Eucharist there is usually little time for her to reflect. How, then, can its phrases come alive? Much depends on the penitential rite. During it, she is invited to look within at her real self, filled with resentment. But if she is not in touch with this anger and resentment, being brought to salvation means little. The words do not fit her experience. She does not see herself in need of being freed, or in need of salvation.

What if she had already wrestled with this unpleasantness and the pull of revenge in personal prayer? At the liturgy, when the presider in the penitential rite invites each worshiper to look within, it would be easy to be in touch with it all: "Lord, present before you now is one who is so reluctant to let go! I know how wrong I am, and how little logic there is in my refusal to forgive, but I can feel how my heart pulls me away from your will."

The woman is ready to respond to this opening prayer. It has a very good chance of striking a chord within. It contains the promise of salvation, now related to her inner wrestling. She is to be saved from this depressing pattern through Jesus.

During the Eucharist, God proclaims many promises repeatedly. But if they are to be heard, they demand honesty. "Yes," says God in effect, "you are angry. You feel how unfair your husband can be and how unfair it is for me to ask you to forgive. I want to bring you into the eternal life of the Son and renew you in his immortal image. I want you to be reborn in Christ. You will come to see the person who is such a problem for you in a very different light. His unfair ways are a sorrow for me, too. And I never take my eyes from him or from you."

Death is always near the surface of God's Word to us. We are unforgiving despite the brevity of our lives. We keep our own death out of our consciousness in day-to-day living. The concealment of death is a factor in our unforgiving behavior. But at the Eucharist, exposed to God's promises, we are invited to hear that ultimate promise: "I will raise you up." Such a sharing in the divine life is where all the other promises of God point us.

Any talk of eternal life reminds us of the inevitable death that we do not wish to think about. To hear Jesus promise to raise us up, we must be willing to hear our death spoken of. Although it does not seem so, to choose not to forgive is really to choose death. Similarly, a spirit of forgiveness and our resurrection are linked. When forgiveness enters our hearts, a seed is planted that is immortal. This is what we ask of God on Friday of the third week in Advent: "Keep us faithful that we may be helped through life and brought to salvation."

Unfortunately, many of the words used in the liturgy—*salvation, redemption, holiness*—can seem irrelevant to daily concerns. In fact, the texts of the liturgy *are* relevant to the day-to-day events of the believer's life, because Christian spirituality is a doorway leading us to a more involved presence in the world. The liturgy is not intended as a moment of peace in a day riddled with anxiety. Rather, it is a school in anxiety-free living and joyful service.

Since we can only experience the liturgy's full power to the degree that we are present, then the words of the liturgy must help us become more aware of our own reality. When this self-presence occurs, then the consolations that have touched us during the liturgy at our most troubled levels will come back to us again during the day's most troubled moments.

There is something about the way we are saved that motivated Jesus to ritualize his salvific act of love. He could have left it just as something to hear about, read about, and remember. But he chose to leave us his loving surrender to death embodied in bread and wine, in word and gesture. His way of drawing us into the attitude of alert waiting and attentive passivity readies us to be touched by him. It is easy to miss the obvious and forget the determined will at work behind the ritual. Jesus' decision to ritualize dominates the Eucharist. The eucharistic rite presents us with God's active determination and the necessarily passive role we play in the drama of redemption. The prayers of the liturgy picture us as weak to the point of despair and invite us to place our confidence in God's love for us.

The underlying spiritual dynamic at work in the liturgy begins with constant reminders of God's promises. A focus on *where we could be* is made specific in God's offer to fill us with the gifts of faith and love. The giving of these two gifts is repeatedly linked to the ritual act of Eucharist. The eucharistic act becomes the supreme moment when the gifts are offered. We are called to be receptive.

The words and actions remind us that this vision of *where we could be* is not intended to encourage us to save ourselves. The ritual makes it clear that we cannot raise ourselves up by our own efforts. The gifts the liturgy offers are available only to those who are willing to leave the world of illusory security, enter the real world, and taste their weakness. Only that which the liturgy ritualizes, the death of Jesus, can save us from our illusions. Finally, the liturgical texts tell us that God has seen our unhappiness, and has chosen to rescue us no matter what the cost. This spiritual dynamic is at the core of the eucharistic event.

To have any impact on the participant, the liturgical words must be filled with content from each one's inner experience. The words can then be heard as the voice of Jesus, and we can experience the strength of his desires in our regard. We can experience God drawing us up into the divine story; we can experience ourselves as part of God's agenda.

In the tenth century, so it is told, a group of barbarian pagans visited Constantinople for the first time and left this account:

> [T]he Greeks led us to the edifices where they worship their God, and we knew not whether we were in heaven or on earth. For on earth there is no splendor or such beauty, and we are at a loss how to describe it. We only know that God dwells there among men, and their service is fairer than the ceremonies of other nations. For we cannot forget that beauty.[1]

We will illustrate this spirituality first in the texts of Ordinary Time* (the weeks between Epiphany and Ash Wednesday, and the season after Pentecost). The texts for other seasons of the church year are much more explicit in their language, and, as a result, it is much easier to see what their thrust is and then connect the words of these liturgies to the realities of our world.

The liturgy is the path out of dull illusion into the glorious truth. The promise of glory is phrased in a wide variety of ways: God intends you to find in his presence light, happiness, and peace (Eucharistic Prayer I, 547); you are to be counted among the chosen (EP I, 544); you are to be enrolled in a royal priesthood; you are to be a citizen of a holy nation, a member of a people set apart by God (Sundays in Ordinary Time I: Preface 29, 431).

Late in his life, Pierre Loti, the French novelist, commented that ever since childhood, he had been waiting for something golden to happen to him. As he neared death, he came to realize that it would never be; it was never meant to be. But in the liturgy, the Christian is being invited to imagine such a golden event. The endless joy that God experiences is promised to us. A day is coming when we will walk fully in God's presence as living, breathing heirs of everlasting life, coheirs with Jesus, in fellowship with the apostles and martyrs. In that day God will share all that God is.

Just as scripture functions as an opportunity to hear God's promises, so does the liturgy. God makes promises to draw us into the future. He seeds our imaginations with images to fill our hearts with anticipation. Perhaps in our joy we cannot believe. Perhaps we doubt or take it all with a grain of salt. That same dynamic is at work in Christian spirituality. Everything begins with God's golden promises. Hearing those promises leads to desire, dissatisfaction, and despair. They are designed to lead us to the gift of trust in God.

What if you find these scriptural promises do not touch you at all? This *can* happen. Here it is important to note two things. First, the

---

*Note: Hereafter all page references to the *Sacramentary* are to the altar edition of the Catholic Book Publishing Co., New York, 1974.

When a *prayer* is referred to as "a," "b," "c," or "d": **a**=Opening Prayer; **b**=Alternate Opening Prayer; **c**=Prayer Over the Gifts; **d**=Prayer after Communion. **"OT"**=Ordinary Time. Also **"EP"**=Eucharistic Prayer.

power of an image rests on *your* imagining. If you do not let the image find its freshness in your own imagination, it will remain dead. Images wear out, but they can be brought back to life. This is the task of the artist within each of us. Some images will be filled with meaning and energy—often they are images from childhood. For example, when the Russian novelist Dostoevsky was in prison, he had moments of great despair. One day he was walking outside in the Siberian cold. Suddenly, he remembered a day when he was nine years old, walking alone in the forest. He heard someone shout "Wolf!" Terrified he ran to a clearing where there was a serf plowing. The man stopped his work and took the boy into his care, calmed his fears, blessed him, and sent him home, assuring him that he would keep him in sight. Dostoevsky recalled how "he smiled at me, gently as a mother."[2]

Jesus tries to link his good news to powerful images like this that each of us has deep within our imaginations. Each of us must do the same: link the God who is here today to the most splendid images in our life. How could we be anxious, awakening in a world in which our mother or father was God? What if the God who is present to us today actually loves us far more than this? We must let the promises of God come in and find these energetic images. We must let them come to life within us.

Second, we are not asked to strain to believe these promises. We must expose ourselves to hearing them and feeling whatever emotion surfaces. God does not need feigned enthusiasm. Honest indifference is better. Even if we are unable to believe the golden promises spontaneously, if we persevere in hearing and wrestling with them, God's work is being accomplished within us.

The more we live in the real world, the more we will experience how incredible the promises are. It is like what the great scientist, Niels Bohr, said of the quantum theory: anyone who wasn't outraged on first hearing about it didn't understand what was being said. So, too, when we find that we believe the good news, it means we have not heard it. It is intrinsically unbelievable, incredible. The more we are willing to experience the incredible nature of the promises, the more seriously we take them. Attending the liturgy is letting ourselves be bombarded by words that speak of a golden world spectacular beyond imagining. Our voices are to be "one with the angels and saints." Our fellowship is to be with the Spirit of God. Christ's riches are to be ours.

For example, picture a middle-aged woman entering a church. She works part-time and is raising three children. The oldest boy is becoming very confused about his life, and it's frightening for her to see. Yesterday, her own brother started a fight with her over nothing, which brought back a lot of their past. He knows how to enrage her, and she can never predict when he will strike. It is into her troubled heart that God desires to pour joy.

Just as Charles, the boy at the boarding school, goes from desolation to joy as the result of a phone call from his mother, so God's voice can transform this woman's experience of life. Into her ears God wishes to speak of glory. She is chosen, set apart. She is being gathered into God. God is determined to flood her existence with life and light. That promise can be her sustenance.

We may feel uncomfortable with these texts of perfect faith and love that the liturgy puts on our lips, but good liturgy invites us to experience the tension between where we are now and where God wants to bring us, clothed with Jesus' faith and love.

Another example: A young man comes into the church. His father, who has been the center of his life, is dying. What does God want him to know, to hear? For him, God has words of endless consolation: his father is to inherit with the saints. He will be raised from death. His place at the paschal feast of heaven is already prepared. Many people are waiting for him. The young man is invited to enter these images and share with God that future scene when he and his father will see each other again face to face. This assurance is the antidote to despair and illusion.

The worshiper hears one golden promise after another. The Father "wants to see and love in us what He sees and loves in Christ" (Sundays in OT VII: Preface 35, 443). We are to be of "one body" with Christ, of "one spirit" (EP III, 554).

This entrance into glory is not something that comes unexpectedly. Rather, the Lord is already preparing us moment by moment for that day when we will be ready for it. As that day nears, God brings us to the fulfillment of love. That "gathering of a people to (himself)" (EP III, 552), which is one of the liturgy's descriptions of human history, is a specific enrichment of that history by the gifts of faith and love.

Promises are usually about the future, but a promise can refer to the present. If what we do now is hidden, we can promise someone that we are doing it now even though it cannot be seen. Many of the liturgical promises refer to present but unperceived actions of God. The coming resurrection from the dead is the flower of seeds already at work. Immortality is being planted deeply in our hearts, and the grave will not be able to keep it down.

The promises assure us that even now God is at work within us, cleansing, purifying, and renewing. A new way of living is invading our old life. God lights up our darkness by invading our consciousness. God wants to deliver us now from all anxiety and to fill our days with joyful waiting. The church prays, "Deliver us from *all* sin and from *all anxiety* [because] we are awaiting the blessed hope and coming of our Savior Jesus Christ" (Order of Mass: Embolism of Lord's Prayer, 562). How little we believe it.

A new way of living in which our consciousness is preoccupied with the future and freed from the illusion of death envelops us precisely because God is making us grow in love and reconciling us to others. God is healing the wounds of sin and division. It may not appear that way as we sit in the pew. This growth of love is not something we can perceive, but we can hear God's voice assuring us that he is indeed drawing us into a new way of experiencing life. God is out to make us eager to serve others so that we can be seated in the banquet hall. God must make us joyful servants of others, for that is to be like God.

Joy is not just our destined future. Joy is to be ours now. Forgiveness can come into our lives. That is the life God has in mind for us, a joy-filled forgiving different from the reluctance to forgive that we often feel. How can God make us eager to forgive?

A counselor was once awakened at midnight by a student with a problem. They talked until six in the morning when they had to stop so the counselor could get ready for work. That afternoon the counselor noticed he was very sleepy but couldn't understand why. Ordinarily he was alert in the afternoon. It was a while before he remembered that he had lost most of the previous night's sleep. It struck him that if it had been any other student who had come, he would have been very conscious of his tiredness and its cause. Perhaps he even would have refused to see the person or would have restricted the chat to a half hour. But for this particular student, he had gladly surrendered his sleep. He did not feel he had been imposed on—if this student needed help, he was glad to supply it, and would even forget how much time he had given him. Instead of spending all day remembering how his kindness had been abused, he had forgotten it. Because he had much affection for this student, he was eager to help.

In the liturgy, Jesus invites us to imagine that he is capable of transforming us into people who readily forgive. The free forgiving that Jesus lived is to be lived in our own lives through a strengthening beyond belief. We will receive the power of affection for those who are unfair to us. We will become like God. Our lives will be sealed with love. We are being made into one family, a circle of endless affection. Jesus calls us to love as he loves and gives us the strength to follow the call (15 OT [b], 304). He is forming our hearts in his love (13 OT [b], 300). We are being drawn into the circle of his life (23 OT [b], 320).

For the revengeful, the resentful, the guilty, there are multiple promises of transformation and renewal. They draw us out of our depressing illusions and bring us into the real world. They may have little grip on us because we are schooled in despair and expect nothing. All Jesus needs from us is that willingness to expose ourselves to his words, to wonder, "What if they are true?"

Our march from illusion to reality begins here. The apostles are not presented in the Gospels as profound believers. But they did not walk away from Jesus. They stayed around and that was enough for God to work with. All God needs is for us to be present when the words about the free gift of divine life are spoken.

To clothe us in immortal life, God must clothe us in immortal love. That is God's assurance to us here and now: "I am entering your heart in ways you do not see. The blood of Jesus in your mouth is a sign of the hidden invasion taking place within your heart. A superior form of loving is entering you and it is deathless."

As God works within our resentful hearts, we begin to behave like the Trinity, although we will not notice it. The precious gift of longing for God's presence more than for life itself comes into our restlessness (21 OT [b], 316). Gradually, the real world of God's loving gains a greater foothold in our consciousness. We become preoccupied with God's desires.

The liturgy, then, is God's way of expanding our hearts with joy (33 OT [b], 340). In the liturgy, God can promise us a share in his life precisely because in the liturgy, the love and faith we need are being made available to us. Seeds of faith and love that will blossom into immortality are being sown through the liturgical action itself. Just as Jesus the carpenter is the full expression of God, so too in the Eucharist, human action and human words carry the weight of a divine event.

How can God's gifts of loving and believing be linked to any particular spoken word or common human gesture? How can the coming into human history of incredible blessedness be linked with a particular rite occurring at a particular time and place? How can any one human being be the meaning of our history?

That transcendent, sacramental world that we find at the heart of Christian spirituality is also at the heart of the liturgy. An action of God is taking place. Just as at the touch of Jesus' hands, sight flowed into blind eyes, so under the material signs of the Eucharist, the immortalizing Spirit is flowing into our hearts.

"By this Eucharist give the true faith continued growth throughout the world" (4 OT [d], 283). "By our sharing in the mystery of this Eucharist, let your saving love grow within us" (15 OT [d], 305). The Eucharist itself makes us one with Christ (20 OT [d], 315) and gives our lives new purpose (16 OT [d], 307). The Eucharist itself makes us holy (17 OT [c], 308). Somehow, the coming of glory into our lives is channeled through the Eucharist (28 OT [c], 330).

By repeatedly including in our prayers this emphasis on the role that Jesus chose for the Eucharist, God constantly calls to our attention that God alone saves. What God does makes the difference between salvation and destruction. In the bread and wine, we have symbols of God's work in Christ. Therefore, we can say that "by the mystery of this bread and wine" we "come to share in the divinity of Christ" (Order of Mass: Prayer at Preparation of Gifts, 371). What power is attributed to bread and wine! Our sharing in divinity has been deliberately linked to bread and wine. It is a call to experience the powerful will of God to save. The working out of God's decision is at the center of the liturgy's focus. All our meaning and our blessed future come to us as a remarkable gift. Through this eating and drinking, we become what God has promised.

Once, because of this divine will, a hand could touch and heal, and a voice could speak and forgive. Now it is a different hand and a different voice, but that same will is at work, pressing itself into the human story. Through these gestures and words, God's kindness becomes present to us and active within us. Because that will is present, the bread and wine effect a salvation that no efforts of our own could deliver.

That will is our sustenance. Without it we falter (11 OT [a], 296). So we ask "to live according to it" (11 OT [a], 296). All of our holiness, our fulfillment of the law, our happiness, comes to us as a gift. "Without you nothing is holy, nothing has value" (17 OT [a], 308). Within that will our "nothing" becomes holy and takes on value. We need to be raised "beyond the limits this world imposes" (Epiphany [b]; 10 OT [b], 294) if we are to enter this new life. The Lord brings us to give up counting on our merits, to forget what we really deserve (EP I, 547), for the coming of this new life and energy is beyond anything we deserve.

What *we* must bring to the liturgy is receptivity. What is receptivity? It's the difference between Zacchaeus (Luke 19:1–10) and the rich young man (Luke 18:18–23). Zacchaeus was receptive and he received Jesus at his table. The rich young man was not a sinner like Zacchaeus. Sinners have great needs. The young man saw Jesus as offering something that was not vital, something extra. Once Zacchaeus was given a glimpse of what Jesus was offering, he knew he had to have it. That's receptivity. It includes a painful awareness of emptiness and the hearing of a promise of fullness.

Our spiritual activities apart from the liturgy have as their goal the fine-tuning of that receptivity which makes it possible for the liturgy to work. Who will be raised up by the Spirit's power and infused with the exaltation that results in joyful gospel living? Those who need it, and those who are aware of that need. Those who want it. Those who expect it to be placed in their open hands because of God's compassion for them. Liturgy has no meaning for those out of touch with their needs.

We must come to the liturgy aware that our faults and weaknesses obscure the vision of glory (3 OT [b], 280) and lock us into despair. We ask God to place the desire for the heavenly gifts in our hearts (22 OT [b], 318), the desire for God's will to absorb each part of our being. We pray, "Increase our faith" (22 OT [a] 318; 9 OT [b] 292). The good news is: freedom and joy are coming, but only to the poor, the captive, and those in sorrow (EP IV, 557).

The universal call to conversion issuing from the Eucharist was a problem for the pagans. Origen describes a pagan named Celsus, an early critic of Christianity, who noticed that those who summon people to religious rites proclaim that the rites are for those with "pure hands and a wise tongue." But, Celsus observes, "let us hear what folk these Christians call. 'Whoever is a sinner,' they say, 'whoever is a child, and, in a word, whoever is a wretch, the Kingdom of God will receive.'"[3]

Today the presider at a Eucharist does the same when he calls us at the beginning of the Eucharist to prepare ourselves to celebrate by acknowledging our failures and calling to mind that we are sinners. For this to mean anything, a person must come to the liturgy in touch with the resentments, the anxieties, the anger, and the lack of desire and expectation that infect each human situation. This is the meaning of the penitential rite. We must bring to the liturgy our honestly acknowledged emptiness.

Just before eating the Lord's flesh and blood, we repeat the penitential rite by affirming our unworthiness and ask to be healed of the wounds that we are beginning to become conscious of. That emptiness of the self is what disposes us for God's action.

Through the sufferings he endured, Jesus restored hope to a fallen world (14 OT [b] 302). This work of restoration becomes present to us in the Eucharist. His sacrifice makes us God's people (21 OT [c] 316). In the Eucharist that death is proclaimed (26 OT [d] 327) and that salvation touches us now: "For when we proclaim the death of the Lord, you continue the work of his redemption" (2 OT [c] 278). The Eucharist's central role in Christian spirituality rests on the presence of Jesus' death. Because of that identity between Jesus' death and the Mass, the effects we attribute to Jesus' dying, freedom from sin and death, the coming of peace and life, are now attributed to the liturgical rite.

In the Eucharist God wills that we be present at an execution. We are accused of leading selfish lives, so selfish that we must be handed over to torturers. The entry of torturers into our lives, as Jesus imagines in the parable of the unforgiving debtor (Matt 18:23–35), may seem to be a bit much. What have we done to deserve such punishment? At worst, we might be aware of a slight lack of forgiveness. We may feel that even this was understandable given the provocation. Surely we do not deserve to be tortured. But the liturgy insists that Jesus' death liberates us. It insists that we need his death. If not for the execution of Jesus, our lives would remain locked in selfishness and a deadening lack of expectation. His death liberates by making the Spirit available to us.

We lead lives that cannot be saved unless God is put to death. Such a message will not take root in us if we are out of touch with our malice. We need help to grow in self-awareness and in amazement at our refusal to forgive. Wars horrify us. Starving children horrify us. But our own way of living and not loving does not horrify us. The murder of Jesus can help us see the malice of our everyday choices. It can help us be more sensitive to the torture we put others through. As consciousness of our refusal to love grows, we become more susceptible to the impact of this murder. It portrays us honestly, but it also exalts us. Our entry into the world of God's precious favors is through a door marked "murderer." Wretches are welcome. At the very moment when the king's messengers are inviting us to the banquet hall, they are revealing to us how savage is our life in the ditch.

It is important to grasp the connection between our sins today and Jesus' execution then. There is something in sin that demands that the culprit be handed over to the torturer. The good news is that we were not handed over to the torturer. One of us, however, was handed over: Jesus, the innocent Son of God. The connection between his death then and our present sin is this: if God is love, then every willful elimination of love is an elimination of the Son of God (EP II, 495).

Because Jesus' unjust execution is made present, each liturgy is a Passover. Our thanksgiving is always linked to blood. By God's design our thanksgiving comes through the sacramental presence of the execution of Jesus, "a death he freely accepted."

Thanksgiving cannot spring from a carefully selective look at the world. If it rises from good health, the lovely weather, the fine food we eat as we forget the agony of our brothers and sisters and our own role in all this pain, it is a word on the lips. The Lord whom we thank looks with undistracted gaze at those who suffer. We must not ask God to forget them for a moment. Any image of God we have that does not include God's sleepless concern for the needy is an idol of our own making. So, too, any liturgy that seeks meaning apart from the execution of Jesus is false worship. Whenever we ritualize, we run the risk of concealing the reality beneath the symbol; a symbol conceals as well as reveals. Recall Kafka's parable, *Leopards in the Temple:*

> Leopards break into the temple and drink the sacrificial chalices dry; this occurs repeatedly, again and again: finally it can be reckoned upon beforehand and becomes a part of the ceremony.[4]

Sacrilege becomes ceremony. We are shocked the first time we see a starving child. By the tenth time, we are immune. We have learned to fit it into our schedule. It has become an undisturbing part of life. The liturgy keeps calling us to the awareness of the seriousness of the death we are living and the life we are called to, to go beneath the level of superficial cheerfulness to true joy and to a passionate love beyond cheap camaraderie or mere courtesy.

The Lord sees the straits we are in: how separated we are from each other by our self-justification. We live with so little joy. Our confidence is so brittle, our needs are so great. The demons of fear and pride are apparently in permanent possession of us. He looks down on us in our moments of need (24 OT [b] 322). He is ever close to us (12 OT [b] 298). He watches over us (5 OT [b] 284). Each thought of ours is guarded by him, each tear is heeded and each joy noticed. (5 OT [b] 284).

In the liturgy, as in any prayer, it is easy to miss the forest for the trees. We can become so attentive to the particular meaning of each detail that we miss the point. The central point is the enlarged experience of God. God is there wanting us to experience his presence. He is eager that we experience him—not only in his words but also in himself.

He especially wants us to encounter him as someone with an agenda, as someone filled with determination to get his way. Jesus' words of the king in the parable are the words of the Father: "I want my banquet hall full!" (Luke 14:23). We use the term *God's will,* but it can fail to suggest the tremendous, even dangerous, energy there. Here is the one who has deliberately drawn us out of nothing. His will is the only difference between us and nothingness. He has not dragged us out of nothingness for drudgery but for glory. A commentary on Ephesians suggests that "the will of God" sounds like a piece of paper left behind after someone dies.[5] It fails to capture the "willfulness" present in God.

The word *decision* is offered in its place. This suggests someone who is powerful, wise, and overwhelming, in a true sense, dangerous. His willfulness leads us to that sharp edge where we must make a decision that spells life or death for us. That is the Person who is present in the eucharistic liturgy. Not to notice that Someone is to miss the point. His willfulness is the energy that has crafted the Eucharist precisely to enable us to encounter him, to experience him in a deeper way.

The central image of the liturgy is not imaginative texts, but the Person addressed. In the liturgy, we keep meeting a God who hovers over us. God's eyes are filled with compassion and the awareness of our pain. God's gaze is that of a loving Father. God is very conscious of where we are, and of where we could be. God is determined to change us in the celebration of the Eucharist.

There is thus a dynamic present in the liturgy that calls us to an awareness of our need and how God responds to that need. The liturgy presupposes a spirituality of receptivity for the gift God holds out to us, and thus it presupposes a habitual monitoring of our choices that reveals our needs and wounds. Because of this self-knowledge, we can put a name on our bad choices in the penitential rite; we can bring our wounds to be cured and emptiness to be filled with the bread and wine at the preparation of the gifts. In the course of the Eucharist our emptiness is transformed like the bread and wine because in the holy communion Jesus' power to love and to believe is planted within us by the Holy Spirit communicated to us in the Eucharist.

This divine determination is the centerpiece of the eucharistic prayers. We are grateful because when we sin and wander far from God's friendship, we are reunited with God through the blood of the Son and the power of the Holy Spirit. God gathers us into the church, calling us to be the people of God praising God in all things. God makes us the Body of Christ and the dwelling place of the Holy Spirit (Sundays in OT VIII: Preface 36, 445).

Jesus enters our story and changes it. By his command to love, he lays on us a burden beyond our ability to carry. He raises our sights to a way of living that is desirable but impossible. He sets a new goal we never could have come to by reason: our becoming a loving people fulfilling an impossible command. It is a dream only God could have dreamed. Then he encourages us to ask for its fulfillment. We are to take for granted that God will give us as a gift what we joyfully glimpse. He teaches us how to pray: "Ask!" And so the church asks:

> May our fulfillment of his command reflect *your* wisdom
> and bring your salvation to the ends of the earth. (6 OT [b] 286)

The new goal *and* its fulfillment are God's doing.

> For our sake he opened his arms on the cross;
> He put an end to death and revealed the resurrection.
> In this he fulfilled *your* will
> and won for you a holy people.
> (Weekdays in OT VI: Preface 42, 457, 548)

Even in our prayer to Jesus, we mention that will:

> Lord Jesus Christ, Son of the living God,
> by the will of the Father.... (Order of Mass, 563)

And it is in this same prayer that work is praised—*God's* work, not ours:

> by the will of the Father
> and the work of the Holy Spirit.... (Order of Mass, 563)

It is that same will of the Father that is being pictured as ever at work, in his Spirit, in Jesus, and in us.

Trust in that divine plan is our way of thanksgiving:

> Open our eyes to your deeds,
> our ears to the sound of your call,
> so that our every act may increase our sharing
> in the life you have offered us. (7 OT [b] 288)

Liturgy is teaching us. It invites us to see ourselves implicated in Jesus' murder, and, in this way, responsible for wars and injustice, for nuclear horror and starving children. We prefer to picture ourselves disassociated from these events. But even in a wedding Mass, it is all present, a jarring note in a joyous gathering. Blood must be shed for us to be healed and for the bride and groom to be able to love.

The liturgy promises exaltation. It urges us to trust as Jesus trusted, and it enables us to do so. We will find that the Lord is always present to our real selves. Our concern for our future is dwarfed by his concern. Our desires for happiness and peace seem shallow, fleeting, and ineffective compared to his total involvement. Even his Beloved's blood will be shed, so precious are we.

Apart from the texts, the gospel is made present in the liturgical gestures. With heads bowed, we become the publican, unworthy to be here, so trivially do we live.

In the pre-Vatican II offertory of the Mass, we made a typical human gesture toward God: we offered God something. In other words, we started a liturgical rite that makes sense to us. In *our* story it is fitting that we offer something of ours to God. It fits our view of things, much like serving the Master at table. It is a proper behavior, and it is instinctive with us. But this view of the offertory reveals how little we grasp the radical nature of the decision God made before the world began. That is why the "offertory" was made simply into a "preparation of the gifts" in the reformed Mass.

God has transformed our story, and our *neediness* is to be the motive of God's actions, not our *worthiness*. He seeks the needy on whom to bestow the Christ. In reality, the rite of the preparation of the gifts is nothing other than an honest expression of our neediness.

After the placing of the bread and wine on the altar, a different story intersects ours. We overhear a conversation that surpasses anything that ever happened in human history. Like Rosencrantz and Guildenstern, we are made part of a larger world. The Father's will and the willing obedience of Jesus become present to us. That determination of the Father to rescue us from our deadly refusal to love finds a full welcome in the willingness of Jesus to shed his blood. The inner heart of God is uncovered as the bread and wine become the flesh and blood of the Christ, the firstborn from the dead. A table is set and a kiss is given. In the presence of such gracious kindness, our unworthiness is underlined. How differently we live and in what darkness we breathe, so ungifted is our waking and sleeping. Such is our sin. But sin makes us needy, and neediness draws God's gaze to us. Now his turning toward us brings food to our mouth.

In *The Lord of the Rings,* the elves provide the hobbits with a cake called "lembas." It stays sweet for many, many days. "One will keep a traveler on his feet for a day of long labor." Now God pours into our mouth the Spirit, and we all drink. It is the very energy of God. How inadequate are our words, worship, sacrifice, even liturgy, for they all have their roots in the human story, an upward act of human beings. How little able are they to describe this glorious gesture of God toward us, a descending act of God. In Christianity those cultic words found in the history of religions are turned inside out.

> Blessed be God the Father of Our Lord Jesus Christ
> He has blessed us with all the spiritual blessings of heaven in Christ.
> Thus he chose us in Christ before the world was made
> to be holy and faultless before him in love
> marking us out for himself beforehand,
> to be adopted children, through Jesus Christ.
> Such was his purpose
> and good pleasure. (Eph 1:3–5)

Chapter Eight

Variations on a Theme

Introductory Note

This chapter seeks to show that the same fundamental spirituality is in each season of the liturgical year. Thus, it will be repetitious. We suggest reading only the section that corresponds to the current liturgical season.

At every Eucharist, the basic message is the same because our basic need is the same: to hear the good news afresh and to receive God's Spirit. The Mass formularies of each liturgical season are a refraction of the same good news seen from the viewpoint of the season being celebrated. Lenten liturgies do not ignore the resurrection; the resurrection is not put on a back burner during the Advent and Christmas cycles.

A. Advent

The golden promises of the risen life that every Eucharist proclaims take on a special form during Advent related to the coming of the Son.

"As we await the coming of your Son" has many meanings. At one level it is a return to the century before the birth of Jesus and to the great expectations that preceded and accompanied his birth. A remarkable atmosphere of hope gripped the Jewish people in those days.

At another level, it refers to his coming to us in glory at the end of human history, when we will share in the divine life at the banquet of heaven and in the resurrection. However, for this glorious resurrection to take place, the Son must come to us now. That coming is what transforms our anger, anxiety, resentment, and fear into the freedom of faith-filled love.

During Advent we ask that the darkness that blinds us to the poisonous nature of unlove will be broken by the light of God's glory shining within us (III Advent Mon [a] 20). We ask God to free us from our slavery to sin (Dec 18 [a], 29) and to provide a new foundation for our lives.

These petitions are based on the promises of God that sustain us in the days that precede Christmas. The Advent liturgies constantly remind us that the heavenly Father is eager for us to hear his promises: "May we come to share the divinity of Christ" (Dec 17 [a], 28). This short phrase that the presider voices contains in itself all the elements of gospel spirituality.

First, there is the incredible promise: "You will share in the divinity of Christ!" Such an image is so far removed from day-to-day routine, so unlikely to happen, that it's not worth dwelling on. It's like a teenager's daydream about a career as a superstar. But the One who makes this promise is the only God. The one and only God has that image of us in mind. Restless until it becomes real, God presses it upon us at every opportunity.

Whenever we hear the Lord's voice as it speaks that golden promise, we experience desire for it and dissatisfaction at our present darkness. We groan at the impossibility of ever getting there. Into our despair comes the Lord's voice: "Ask, and you shall receive!" This is the posture God wants us to take. In the Advent prayer, that is the posture we take as we ask: "May we come to share in the divinity of Christ!" (Dec 17 [a] 28).

As the presider at the assembly prays, we are invited to ask God for a gift we cannot believe in. We are invited into the profound mixture of unbelief and desire, determination and helplessness that make up the prayer of the heart. Authentic liturgy invites us to submit to this tension, to enter it, to be it.

Every promise made in the Advent liturgies sets in motion the fundamental dynamic of gospel spirituality. But it will remain unfelt unless we are in touch with our need of salvation and with God's kindly will. When the basic reality of our need and the heavenly Father's concern is lost, no promises will touch us.

The liturgical texts of Advent also insist that we fix our attention on the central role that the Eucharist plays in our relationship with God. They affirm that the power of God's action is located *in* the eucharistic mystery. The golden promises are all attached to "sharing in the mystery" (I Advent: Tues [d], 5). In text after text, we are invited to believe that "by sharing in the mystery," we will be taught to judge wisely the things of Earth, to love the things of heaven. Through the Eucharist we are prepared for eternal life by the renewing power of the bread from heaven. The Eucharist nourishes us, strengthens us, protects us.

The poisons that infect our freedom—animosity, malice, deeply rooted competitiveness—are touched by the mystery, and we are freed from them and from our inability to believe in the good news. Our communion in the Eucharist teaches us to love heaven. Our lack of interest in the promise of the resurrection is changed by the power of God present in the Eucharist. Our need for revenge is drawn out of us by the sacrament.

The bread and wine become our salvation. We are present at a rescue mission that means little to those who are unaware that they are drowning. The experience of being overwhelmed by unlove makes us want to reach out for the promises of God.

This constant focus on the power in the eucharistic action serves a central purpose. It keeps before us the will, the desires, and the decisions of God. The Eucharist gives God a medium through which the desires of the divine heart and God's way of saving us can be expressed with clarity. The presence of that greatest gift, the body and blood of Jesus in his living sacrifice, draws our attention away from our own efforts and focuses it on the invasion of our story by this One so much more powerful.

The tremendous energy of "that mighty strength" (Eph 1:19) moves into our story, as the bread and wine becomes the divine flesh and blood. The Spirit is given. A new way of living—living because of Jesus—enters our lives as we eat. We are not whipped, tortured, bloodied, martyred, and then rewarded with God's life. Rather, we are fed, and all our attention is on the one who feeds us so splendidly. What a glorious decision of God! What a spectacular will is now the foundation of our happiness!

These golden words are inaudible for those who refuse to be honest. Our lack of interest in the poor, our reluctance to forgive, our fear of the future, our dread of death must be allowed to rise from their hiding places and be exposed. "We are nothing without you" (I Advent: Tues [c], 5). This is a common refrain in this season.

Granted that what God brings to the Eucharist is what counts, what can we bring to it? Confidence in God's love for us is a prerequisite for receiving God's gifts. When we ask for the Spirit with no expectation that the Spirit will be given, we pray uselessly. Whenever we lack that expectation, we must ask God for it. It is the gift of faith. During the Advent season, *readiness* is stressed. We are asked to have a sense of great expectation.

> Lord our God,
> grant that we may be ready
> to receive Christ when He comes in glory
> and to share in the banquet of Heaven. (I Advent: Wed [a], 6)

Even though it is Advent, death comes to mind, for we ask to be filled with readiness for eternal life. How little we want to hear about death and resurrection when we are angry. The horizon of eternal value is swallowed up in today's torment. The message of Advent and the Eucharist is, "All this can be changed." God can touch our lives now and raise us up from discouragement at our weakness. God can help us to look forward with confidence to await the healing power of Christ (II Advent: Wed [a], 14). God can help us to follow the example of Mary, always ready to do God's will (Dec 20 [a], 31).

The dispositions we need in order to enter the eucharistic action effectively are divine gifts. In the Eucharist we are invited to ask for confidence in God's working (II Advent: Fri [a], 16) and to ask for a desire for God's gifts, even to desire that power to forgive the unfairness of others that we may not want at all.

"May He find us waiting, eager in joyful prayer" (I Advent: Mon [a], 4). We ask for a waiting posture in which our attention will be fixed on God, from whom we expect deliverance. We ask to yearn for Christ's coming. These elements of desire and expectation are vital ingredients for effective prayer, and they are gifts of God. Jesus saves us by sharing with us his great desire and unshakeable faith. When these two gifts are accompanied by the awareness of our need, we are enabled to focus on what God is doing. Our salvation consists in being caught up in what God does. When we go to ask a favor of someone, if we know that this person can grant it and will be glad to do it, the asking is easy and untroubled. When we ask God for the gift of desire, we can be certain that he is eager to give, and our asking will be filled with joy.

In the Eucharist, we have "the perfect form of worship" (Dec 23 [c], 34). It is most effective in keeping our gaze fixed on *God's* doings, *God's* desires, *God's* will.

> Lord,
> may this sacrifice
> bring us into the eternal life of your Son,
> who died to save us from death. (Dec 18 [c], 29)

The prayers of Advent repeatedly call to mind the salvific death of Jesus and present it as the centerpiece of the Father's salvific will. They remind us of what God gazes at in the world: our slavery to sin and the crucifixion of his Son.

God sees us in the grip of the ancient powers of sin and death. Advent liturgies call to mind our history: wars and unbreakable injustice. A man can spend in one night of entertainment what would feed a mother and her six hungry children for a month. Our finest young minds are co-opted into producing weapons of total destruction. We resent our brother for weeks at a time. We breathe in darkness, we sleep in darkness, we live in darkness. Below the surface of our awareness, there is always the oncoming of death.

"You decreed and your Word became man" (Dec 17 [a], 28). Long ago, God formed a plan to open a path for us. The Father's love for us was so great that he gave his beloved Son to free us. In Christ we can recognize the unveiling of God's love, and this can fill our hearts with joy.

God has decided to renew humanity and has chosen us to become the new creation, a people like God with our eyes open to the pain of the world and the unshakeable grip unlove has on us, and yet confident in God's loving kindness toward us.

Through greater honesty, we are led during the Advent season toward the coming of the Spirit into our hearts today, and in the gifts of believing and forgiving, toward a greater imprinting of our lives by the coming resurrection.

B. Christmas and Epiphany

The Christmas season, with its secular trappings, challenges gospel spirituality. The focus on the Baby Jesus can easily lose its connection with the essential dynamic of promise, desire, dissatisfaction, despair, and petition. The core eucharistic action can be overshadowed by seasonal devotional elements. Each year preachers struggle to uncover the basic gospel that lies beneath. An indication of the problem is the frequency of sermons on "The True Meaning of Christmas."

The season's theme is that "a child is given to us." That is only the first moment in a lifelong event. The Eucharist celebrates the totality, and re-presents the final climactic moments, when the human will of the Messiah reached its fullness. Therefore, the "child given to us" must be located within God's gift of a redeemer. The invasion of our history by a divine child must be seen against the background of God's decision to intervene and save us from our misuse of our free will.

The ancient prayer that we pray on December 17 and at the preparation of the gifts in each liturgy expresses the connection well:

> May we come to share the divinity of Christ,
> who humbled himself to share our human nature.

Here again is the great promise: sharing the divine nature. Such promises are found throughout the Christmas liturgies.

We are called to be a forgiving people. We are promised that God will enable us to answer that call:

> May the power of his divinity
> help us answer his call to forgiveness and life.
> (Vigil of Christmas [b], 38)

That command to be forgiving is not a summons to reluctant, superficial lip service, but to heartfelt eagerness to obey. This is often not within us, and so we must ask.

> Give us a foretaste
> of the joy that you will grant us
> when the fullness of his glory
> has filled the earth. (Christmas: Mass at Midnight [b], 40)

> May he fill you with joy
> and make you heralds of his Gospel.
> (Christmas: Mass during the Day: Solemn Blessing, 45)

That glimpse of ourselves as joyfully forgiving people can arouse desire in us. God's dream of what our daily life could be like becomes our own dream. It also reveals the wide chasm between us and such happiness. We become conscious of how far we are from living this way.

> Lord, you care for your people
> even when they stray.
> Grant us a complete change of heart,
> so that we may follow you with greater fidelity.
> (Holy Family Sun: Solemn Blessing, 47)

What is not explicit in the liturgies of this season is the despair that recurs in the Christian's spiritual experience. There are references to darkness. There is a mention of our slavery to sin. While we are being invited to ask for deliverance from this slavery, which seems to suggest that it is our present state, the prayer adds a note of ambiguity. It's like saying, "Free me from my former boss." Is it a confusion, or a brilliant effort to present the "already but not yet" tension of Christian existence?

> All-powerful God,
> may the human birth of your Son
> free us from our *former* slavery to sin.
> (Christmas Octave: 6th Day [a], 52)

We pray that the Lord will "draw us beyond the limits which this world imposes" (Epiphany [b], 64). The very engaging in endless petition presupposes the vast weakness within.

While the sense of despair at our human weakness is strongly present in the Christmas liturgies, it is never spelled out explicitly. Just as despair is a necessary step on the path to receptivity in each individual life, so, too, the season that celebrates the supreme gift of the Christ Child presupposes the helplessness in the history of our race.

When we turn to the central role of liturgy, the texts are abundant.

> May we receive the gift of divine life
> through these offerings here on earth.
> (Christmas: Mass at Dawn [c] 42)

On the feast of St. John, we pray that "through this Eucharist" God's Son may "always live in us" (Dec 27 [d], 49). Even the power to fulfill the Love Command is recognized as an effect of the eucharistic action.

> By sharing in this Eucharist
> may we come to live more fully
> the love we profess. (Christmas Octave: 6th Day [c], 52)

The reception of the gifts is linked to the eucharistic act. The opening of our eyes that occurs with the coming of the Baby Jesus is attributed to the rite. On the feast of St. John we ask to share "in the hidden wisdom of your Eternal Word which you reveal at this eucharistic table" (Dec 27th [c], 49).

There is much pressure on us to be happy during this season. The liturgies themselves seem to demand it. "Rejoice! Again I say: rejoice!" Despair seems unwelcome. When we feel it in prayer, we might repress it quickly as inappropriate. But despair is the very place into which the Christ Child is born. For those who choose not to experience their despair, there is no gift. There is just an effort-filled slavery to an illusory self-image. But into the despair within us comes the great promise: "The Godhead is being given to you. Ask for it."

> May we who share his humanity
> come to share his divinity. (Baptism of the Lord [c], 72)

C. Lent

During Lent, the church prepares for the central event of the liturgical year, the celebrations of Holy Week and the Paschal Triduum. The preparation begins with the constant affirmation of God's promises.

The heavenly Father waits for the day when we will live with the Risen Christ. He has promised this inheritance. Our shallow belief in the spectacular will of God must be changed. The Father is determined to make us fully aware of the redemption we have received (III Lent: Fri [d], 104).

Any share in the divine life must be preceded by other gifts. We must put on the likeness of our Lord in heaven (V Lent: Sun [a], 114). By a new birth we become members of God's family. A new heart is being formed within us, a new heart that will produce strength for our weariness and courage when we falter.

Here is the central promise:

> Father of mercy and power,
> we thank you for nourishing us
> with the body and blood of Christ
> and for calling us to share in his divine life.
> (V Lent: Sat [d], 121)

The most incredible promise is to share God's own life. But many glorious promises abound in the eucharistic liturgies of Lent. They invite us to dwell on our incredible future. The risen life is held up before us. The path to this risen life is spelled out: heartfelt repentance and pardon for sin, ready forgiveness of others, deepening of our own faith and love.

> Father,
> You increase our faith and hope,
> You deepen our love in this communion.
> (I Lent: Sun [d], 83)

During Lent, one element is stressed almost every day: *through the Eucharist,* God's healing, energizing Spirit touches us.

Through this sacrament
may we rejoice in your healing power
and experience your saving love in mind and body.
(I Lent: Mon [d], 84)

And in this striking prayer, the Eucharist becomes a synonym for God:

May this Eucharist forgive our sins,
make us holy,
and prepare us for the eternal life you promise.
(III Lent: Wed [d], 102)

Jesus' decision to use bread and wine, human words and human gestures, as the vehicle of his salvific love is repeated in an endless variety of forms. The eucharistic action gives visibility to that invisible will of the Father that is the foundation of our blessedness. "In this Eucharist, we pass from death to life" (IV Lent: Fri [d], 112). We believe that life is coming to us because of God's love for us. The heavenly Father wills it, and so it happens. But in the sacramental act God's will is completely present. The rite itself can bring about what the Father wills.

In text after text this is stressed. God's energy is loosed upon the world, and the sacraments, especially the Eucharist, are the means God uses. Just as we give thanks for the Father's love for us that brings us here on earth a share in the life to come, so, too,

We give thanks for *these holy mysteries*
which bring us here on earth
a share in the life to come. (II Lent: Sun [d], 91)

Our new life has been won for us by Jesus' death on the cross:

Father in Heaven,
the love of your Son led him to accept
the suffering of the cross
that his brothers [and sisters] might glory in new life.
(V Lent: Sun V [b], 114)

It is so easy to look for our salvation in our activity, in sincere efforts that we call to mind whenever we appear to be condemned. We may think, "At least I can say I tried. That's all the Lord can want." Not so! God wants us to be absorbed in the glorious love revealed on the cross, and God offers us that "being-absorbed" as a gift.

> All-powerful God
> the Eucharist proclaims the death of your Son.
> Increase our faith in its saving power
> and strengthen our hope in the life it promises.
> (Wed of Holy Week [d], 130)

The Lenten Eucharists invite us to take a realistic look at our weakness. We are slaves of sin (II Lent: Wed [c], 94). Without God, we are bound to fail (III Lent Mon [a], 100). We are wounded by sin and selfishness. Any rising out of our human weakness and escape from our enslavement to sin can occur because of the decision inside the powerful, wise, and holy God, the decision to save us all. On that our lives depend. There is no meaning for us apart from it.

> Father,
> in your plan of salvation
> your Son Jesus Christ accepted the Cross
> and freed us from the power of the enemy.
> (Wed of Holy Week [a], 130)

That the initiative is God's resounds in the texts. God is ever working. Our Father has given us a savior; he has reached out to us with loving power and restored us to life. God has saved us all from death.

We come to the Eucharist distracted, worried, perhaps angry or resentful. Maybe we seek a moment of peace apart from the struggle. The Eucharist will draw us into reality. We will be reminded of the greater evils that threaten us. We may encounter our lack of interest in God's promises as they are proclaimed in the texts. We need not bring to the Eucharist great depth of faith, but rather our emptiness and need of faith. We may feel no strong faith in these promises but we allow them to be spoken again in our ears.

It is not that we come filled with faith, but that Jesus comes to the Eucharist with his unwavering faith in the Father. His faith is so great that it is enough for us. At the Eucharist we are the church at prayer. When the church is at prayer, its faith in the promises of God is abundant, because when the church is at the Eucharist, Jesus joins us to himself. His bold, full faith is linked to our anxiety.

There is a parallel in Christian action. Christians need not bring to the poor or to the enemy any consciousness of loving them. There may be reluctance. But Christians do not turn away, but instead continue to go to the poor and the needy, trusting in the love that God secretly presses into their hearts.

When we come to the Eucharist, we first define ourselves in honesty. We enter our own presence. If there is no honesty in our lives, we will miss the first step. We will be present at the Eucharist but absent to ourselves. The penitential rite is the liturgical moment of truth. It is not designed for long soul searching. It is intended as a quick entry into the negative self. If that entry does not take place, we will not be ready to celebrate the Eucharist. If we feel our sinfulness only as a general statement rather than a sensed presence of malice, the Eucharist will not touch us.

But if we are free enough to see ourselves realistically, we will encounter indifference to the ritual and to our neighbor. The goal of spiritual activity is to be steadily in touch with that indifference. The promises we expose ourselves to during the readings will both draw us and illuminate our darkness. Light and darkness will intensify and we will be ready to hear about the spectacular decision of the Father. We will be drawn into the other story, where all that is alive circles around the divine decision to make us the recipients of an endless giving. Here is a goodness that overmatches our emptiness and indifference.

In the flesh and blood of Jesus made present when his sacrifice is re-presented to us, we find medicine that operates at a level of reality far deeper than even our terrible wounds.

D. Holy Thursday and Good Friday

On Holy Thursday our attention is centered on Jesus' decision to ritualize his coming death. The new life that would be won for us in his voluntary death is linked by him to a ritual supper.

> Almighty God,
> we receive new life
> from the supper your Son gave us
> in this world. (Holy Thursday [d], 139)

The promise contained in the words *new life* are particularized throughout the liturgy. We are reminded of the great promise, eternal happiness with God, in the second part of the Prayer after Communion.

> May we find full contentment
> in the meal we hope to share
> in your eternal kingdom.

We are invited to look up from our slavery to unlove and see our future, the fullness of love and life (Holy Thursday [a], 136). We are to go from weakness to strength, from uncleanliness to being washed clean (Holy Thursday: Preface 47, 467).

What if the participant cannot feel any reality in these promises? This can lead to entrance into the heart of the redemption event: the faith act of Jesus is offered. The willingness to experience our unbelief will lead to receiving the great gift of faith.

On Holy Thursday and Good Friday the ritual actions are dramatic. In order to keep them from leading us down a devotional detour, it is vital to be conscious of how God is at work within our hearts. Prayer demands sensitivity to God, just as in any dialogue sensitivity to the concerns of the other person is necessary for an effective conversation.

Our Father dreams of the day when we shall "put on the likeness" of Christ in heaven (Good Friday [b], 140). Our resurrection is uppermost in God's mind. Because of our fear of death, our risen life is not our favorite daydream. But if we are willing to accept the fact that God *is* constantly caught up in it, we will be able to dialogue effectively. Our willingness to let God be who he is, is enough for true prayer, even if we do not share God's concerns. When we create the image of a god who never reminds us of the risen life, then we lose touch with the God revealed in Jesus.

The General Intercessions that conclude the liturgy of the Word on Good Friday are splendid reminders of the promises of God. This extraordinary and lengthy series of prayers is often thought repetitious and boring, especially if we lose sight of the presence of a determined God with a determined will. Instead of it being a rich experience of assurance-filled asking for every blessing in the heavens, it becomes a meaningless endurance test. This simple type of petition requires deep faith; the boredom we may experience is a sign of our lack of expectation.

For this prayer to become the experience of God it is intended to be, we first have to taste our lack of faith. Our despair can lead us to ask that God fill us with great expectations and a confident assurance that our prayers will be answered. With that element in place, the repetitious prayers can be a most intense experience of who we are and who God is.

Our heavenly Father is present, filled with desires. His heart is set on guiding the church, helping it to persevere in faith, proclaim his name, and bring his salvation to people everywhere (General Intercessions 1, 142). God cares deeply that each of us receives his help in our vocation and do his work more faithfully (General Intercessions 3, 143). God desires to make all Christians one in a fullness of faith and a fellowship of love (General Intercessions 5, 145). These Good Friday prayers are a litany of God's desires and his gifts.

God has an intense desire that those who do not believe in him may recognize in the lives of Christians the tokens of his love and mercy (General Intercessions 8, 148). His heart is determined to comfort the dying, to free those unjustly deprived of liberty, and to rid the world of falsehood, hunger, and disease (General Intercessions 10, 150).

Good Friday is so focused on Jesus' death on Calvary two thousand years ago that the power of the daily Eucharist is mentioned only indirectly. The Good Friday liturgy is a continuation of Holy Thursday's liturgy. There is no new recalling of the words of Jesus at the Last Supper. The communion in his flesh and blood depends on the previous liturgy, and the two form a unique, single event just as the Last Supper and the crucifixion went from one evening to another.

E. Easter

When we think of the spiritual life in stages such as purgative, illuminative, and unitive, there is a danger of visualizing them as if they occur in succession, rather than all being present all the time. So, too, there is a danger in the liturgical year that one season may lose vital elements of the full liturgical experience. To prevent that from happening during Lent, conscious focus is placed on the resurrection of Jesus: each Lenten Eucharist is a celebration of Jesus' resurrection.

In the Easter season, there may be a temptation to minimize or even ignore the horror in which many live and our indifference to that reality. In our desire to be joyful, we may be tempted to rest from looking at the sufferings of our brothers and sisters, and to postpone further entry into our unlove and unfaith.

The Easter joy born of Jesus' resurrection does not come from any lessening of honesty. In fact, that splendid Easter gift of joy cannot take root when we turn away from the pain of our neighbor's life. Even on Easter morning, children starve and their horrified parents weep bitter tears. Even as we receive the Easter Eucharist, they starve and God gazes at them with undistracted love. We must not try to force the Lord to ignore this. God will not be silent. The Easter joy God brings will enlarge our hearts to embrace what he embraces.

At the very beginning of each Easter Eucharist, we will be invited into the world of personal dishonesty, faithlessness, and lovelessness. If we come to the Eucharist after turning away from the wretchedness of the poor and the depths of dishonesty within us, we will not enter into the Eucharist. Easter draws its meaning from what God wants to do for us. God brings to the eucharistic encounter with us a great desire to heal our hearts into forgiving and concern.

The resurrection's joy can enlarge its grip on our consciousness only when our sensitivity to the needs of others is enlarged, only when we become more like the Lord. But if we come to the Easter Eucharist determined to keep out any depressing thoughts, we will prevent God from accomplishing his goal. If our spiritual life has been effective and we move along a path of growing honesty, we will find it easy to be honest during the penitential rite. We will readily become conscious of that part of us that is turned away from reality and love so vigorously. The eucharistic celebration will then surround us with an incense cloud of promises, God's promises, the good news.

"You are to live with me forever" (Ash Wednesday: Blessing of the Ashes, alternate prayer, 77; also Easter Vigil: Blessing of the New Fire, opening prayer, 171). It is as if God says, "I am hard at work filling you with trust in me and with a heartfelt concern for your brothers and sisters."

During the eucharistic celebration, the air will be filled with voices assuring us that this ritual action in which we partake is filled with mighty power. The liturgical action itself has become, through Jesus' choice, the instrument of God's will to transform us into a faith-filled, forgiving people.

In place of building by our own efforts, voices will invite us to be expectant and aware of our great need for God's intervention. The voices will lead us toward an intensified receptivity. Then we will be ready to become the objects of God's costly healing. The Eucharist will bring us in touch with the endless energy that filled Jesus as he offered his life for us. His never-changing will encounters our coldness, inertia, fear, and indifference. We enter into the story in which our wretchedness has been seen by a loving friend, and we have been given a servant who washes us in his very blood "which is immortal love" (Ignatius of Antioch, *Letter to Romans*).[1] And so, anyone who needs bread will become our focus. Anyone who needs forgiveness will be our concern. Salvation history, God's story, will be enacted within us.

Let us look at the promises of Easter. In the opening prayer of the Easter Vigil (p. 171) we hear:

> [I]f we honor the memory of his death and resurrection
> by hearing his word and celebrating his mysteries,
> then we may be confident
> that we shall share his victory over death
> and live with him forever in God.

Great promises are attached to eucharistic participation. It is not magic that brings this about. God's effective will informs the words and gestures with power beyond our human reckoning. Great things are promised:

> Father,
> *in this Eucharist*
> we touch the divine life you give to the world.
> (Ascension [d], 261)

The Eucharist helps us to grow in love (IV Easter: Sat [d] 241). It makes our faith stronger (VII Easter: Fri [a], 268). We are inflamed with hope (Easter Vigil: Blessing of the Fire, 171). All evil and guilt are washed away (*Exultet,* para. 4, 184).

How easy it is not to believe that we are to be forgiven with a word. When our sense of guilt is shallow, we find it is quite easy to believe this, but not important or consoling. But if we become conscious of the comfort and security we enjoy on the same planet where our brothers and sisters suffer, and if we are conscious of how unforgivable is our refusal to love and forgive others, then we will hear an incredible word: "Nevertheless, your sins are washed away." If all we ever bring to the Lord are easily forgivable sins, how will we ever hear his most consoling words; how will we ever come to know him in his most bold loving?

We are to become, according to God's promises, children confident to call him Father (II Easter: Mon [a], 220), people who express in our lives the love we celebrate (IV Easter: Sun [a], 256). The love we celebrate is to become through God's promise our daily practice (VII Easter: Sun [a], 269).

> Lord,
> may this sharing in the sacrament of your Son
> free us from our old life of sin
> and make us your new creation. (Easter Wed, [d], 214)

We are to feel its saving power in our lives (II Easter: Thurs [d], 223). We are to know the strength of God's outstretched arms (IV Easter: Sun IV [b], 234).

> The Redeemer has given you lasting freedom.
> May you inherit his everlasting life.
> (VI Easter: Sun, Solemn Blessing, 251)

It is now that God seeds us with faith and love. In the future these seeds will blossom into everlasting life. The hope of the resurrection is to fill us (II Easter: Wed [a], 222) so that our consciousness never ceases to look forward.

> May our mortal lives be crowned with the ultimate joy
> of rising with him
> who is Lord for ever and ever. (VI Easter: Sun [b], 250)

Because these promises are being fulfilled sacramentally, we do not yet see, and we are still called to believe in God's Word, to believe that God is at work in these sacramental mysteries. It is because in the Eucharist the Spirit gives us the power to love and believe that we can pray:

> Lord, may our participation in this Eucharist
> increase your life within us,
> cleanse us from sin,
> and make us increasingly worthy of this holy sacrament.
> (VII Easter: Wed [d], 226)

As we pray at the blessing of the water in the Easter Vigil: "Father, you give us grace through sacramental signs" (para. 1, p. 201), it may not be obvious to us why God has chosen to channel divine energy through ritual and sacrament. But so it is: bread and wine, word and gesture are the means God uses to convey grace, God's energizing life, just as it is conveyed through water at the Easter Vigil:

> By the power of the Spirit
> give to the water of this font
> the grace of your Son. (Blessing of the Water, para 3, 202)

In our desire to avoid any misunderstanding about the appearance of magic, we must not deemphasize the true presence of God's powerful will in the sacrament. It was Jesus who chose to ritualize his voluntary dying. Of the blessed water we say:

> You have made of it a servant of your loving kindness.
> (Blessing of the Water, para 2, 203)

So, too, the Lord has chosen to touch us in the Eucharist, not just with inner assurances, but also with visible shapes and gestures and audible voices, with what can be felt and eaten and tasted. "He who eats me, the same also shall live because of me" (John 6:57). Our salvation is primarily something being done to us. The sacramental ritual keeps our focus on *God's* will and calls upon us to let *God* save us.

For one who participates in the Eucharist solidly grounded in the humility that comes from self-knowledge, the attention the liturgy gives to God's decisions and saving action is good news indeed. To be aware of the strength of unlove's grip is the best preparation for hearing the invitation of the ritual to trust not in anything within the self, nor to seek a justification for life in some reasonable decent past history, but rather to rest quite naked in the arms of the Lord.

> [W]ithout your Spirit
> [we] could never raise [our] voice
> in words of peace. (Pentecost: Mass During the Day [b], 272)

In other words, we cannot say the loving word, we cannot love without his power. We can come up with a deceptive substitute, of course—the kind word that tries to mask the heart. But the truly loving word is beyond our power to speak because the truly loving heart must be given to us first.

> Without your Spirit
> man could never raise his voice in words of peace
> or announce the truth that Jesus is Lord....
>   (Pentecost: Mass During the Day [b], 272)

Hearing the gospel is not enough to save us, for we are too fearful to believe it. Only God's Spirit flowing into us can enable us to say in truth, "I believe." We rest on his inspiration. We bring him an emptiness to fill (IV Easter: Wed [a], 238).

> He is the glory of the humble, of the honest.
> (IV Easter: Wed [a], 238)

> Make our faith strong and our hope sure.
> May we never doubt that you will fulfill
> the promises you have made. (V Easter: Tues [a], 245)

The passage into that happy state where we never doubt his promises can take place only through his suffering and death (Octave of Easter: Fri [d], 216). That costly purchase is not downplayed in the Easter season:

> By the suffering, death, and resurrection of your Son
> may we come to eternal joy. (IV Easter: Sat [a], 241)

Even the wounds of Jesus are recalled. As he inserts the five grains of incense in the paschal candle, the principal celebrant says:

> By his holy
> and glorious wounds
> may Christ our Lord
> guard us
> and keep us. Amen.
> (Easter Vigil: Preparation of the Candle, 172)

The words, the gestures, the bread, the wine, the water, the fire— each becomes a servant of God's loving kindness. Through these sensible realities we are in contact with that loving will, the centerpiece of our history and the reality at the heart of the Eucharist. It is a will to transform us, to clothe us with a new way of living and with divine instincts, a divine pattern of loving.

But part of our reality is yet unredeemed. "Inasmuch as we are selfish and shut in ourselves, we are before Christ."[2] Part of us has not heard the gospel. When Ignatius of Antioch wrote to the Smyrneans about some "who care not for love, nor for the widow, the orphan, the oppressed, those who are in prison or have been released, nor for those who are in hunger and thirst," he was describing a part of each of us, the part untouched by Christ.[3] It is on this that God's salvific gaze focuses as we enter God's presence. To be exposed to Jesus' flesh and blood is to touch the determination that inflames the Father who has made Jesus the sacrament of his own desire and who insists, "I want my banquet hall full" (Luke 14:23). Jesus was conscious of that will. He saw his life and mission as an expression of his Father's heart.

The new creation, the life in the full light of truth that the Father has destined for us, requires a bath in the cleansing waters of self-knowledge. We can be redeemed only to the extent to which we see ourselves.

God's will and determination come up against our demand to be declared innocent, to be acknowledged as basically decent, cooperative people, not really responsible for the wretchedness of the poor. Take, for example, this picture of a true believer from Ceslaus Spicq's *Agape in the New Testament:* "In a world of the rich, the well-fed, the merry, and the admired, the members of God's Kingdom will appear as poor,

hungry and wretched."[4] How far we are from being in the kingdom!
How badly we need a deeper honesty to illuminate our poverty and our
helplessness! Only then can we become children and place our trust in
God's loving kindness and thereby enter God's kingdom.

The Easter Eucharists present us with an image of human history
as dark as any existentialist would devise. It is a fallen world, filled
with division (Pentecost: Vigil Mass [b], 270). Christ enters a "broken
world" where sin has had a long reign (Easter: Preface IV, 421). Before
Christ we are a people whose hearts and minds are darkness, whose
lives drag along chained by death (*Exultet,* 183). There is misery
(V Easter: Thurs [a], 247) and despair (Easter Sunday [b], 208).

> What good would life have been to us,
> had Christ not come as our Redeemer? (*Exultet,* 183)

But God has opened and holds open for us the way to eternal life
(VII Easter: Fri [a], 268). Through no merit of ours but by a willful
decision of God, the Son is given away and the slave is ransomed
(*Exultet,* 183).

> Most blessed of all nights, chosen by God
> to see Christ rising from the dead! (*Exultet,* 184)

The revivifying of Christ's wounded body was the event around
which human history would revolve. The Father has found a way to
center our attention on his Beloved Son and on his human freedom. In
Jesus the Father found a way of fully expressing his desires.

> Father, how wonderful your care for us.
> How boundless your merciful love. (*Exultet,* 183)

The fifty days of Easter celebrate the fullness of the mystery of
his revealed love (Pentecost: Vigil Mass [b], 270) In glorifying Christ,
the Father has opened our path to eternal life (Easter Sunday [a], 208).

Chapter Nine

The Liturgy of the Word

Jesus did not intend to liberate Israel from Rome, but from "the sover-eignties and the powers who originate the darkness in this world, the spiritual army of evil in the heavens" (Eph 6:12, *NJB*). God's instrument of liberation would not be military support, but the gift of God's own energy, his very Spirit. The power to love and to believe as Jesus himself loved and believed would bring victory over the army of evil.

As he became conscious of his approaching death, Jesus saw that his preaching alone would not succeed, and he turned to ritual. That supper ritual embodied his message of liberation and the gift of the Spirit in a way that words could not.

Throughout this study, we have been deriving the principles of spirituality from the Gospels. In this chapter we explore how this spiri-tuality can help us to understand the role of the liturgy of the Word in the Mass, how the readings and the homily can lead to fuller participa-tion in the eucharistic ritual. We reflect on the nature of the homily according to the mind of the church today: how the homily can and should be a privileged means of spiritual formation and direction for the congregation. We conclude with some thoughts on how Christians can effectively prepare themselves "to celebrate the Sacred Mysteries."

In chapter eight we used the texts of the *Sacramentary* to illus-trate the principles of gospel spirituality at work in the liturgy. In this chapter we focus on what the homilist can do with the *Lectionary* texts for each Sunday and weekday. Many books are available that help the preacher prepare the Sunday homilies. These books usually take each Sunday in turn. Our goal is somewhat different: we hope to show that a homilist who has grasped the principles of gospel spirituality can use any *Lectionary* text more effectively. Gospel spirituality can bring vitality to his Sunday and weekday homilies when their principles are recognized in the scripture texts of any day.

For some priests preaching is a burden. Each Sunday the priest *has* to say something but often *has nothing to say* that springs from the scripture readings and touches people's lives by offering challenge and hope. We try to show how the spirituality implicit in the entire New Testament and refracted through the texts of the day will give him much that will enrich the lives of his people and at the same time enrich and foster the holiness of the priest-homilist himself.

We necessarily must focus on the priest as opposed to the general Christian public for whom this book was also written, because the priest is the one who presides over the liturgy of the Word and preaches within it. However, there are serious implications here for laypeople who are seeking to integrate personal spirituality with liturgy. We explicate this later in the chapter.

The *Constitution on the Sacred Liturgy* (52) states "The homily…is to be highly esteemed as part of the liturgy itself; and again:

> …a sermon is part of the liturgical action….The sermon, moreover, should draw its content mainly from scriptural and liturgical sources, for it is the proclamation of God's wonderful works in the history of salvation, which is the mystery of Christ ever made present and active in us, especially in the celebration of the liturgy. (*Constitution on the Sacred Liturgy,* 35)

In the early church this was common practice. St. Justin, in his *First Apology* (A.D. 165), captures the integrality of scripture and homily: "When the reader has finished the president of the assembly verbally admonishes and invites all to imitate the splendid things we have just heard [in the reading]."[1] Thus for Justin the homily emerges from the readings. This idea was lost in the medieval period and was only restored by Vatican II.

Vatican II insisted that the homily was to be tied to the scripture readings. But the homily must also link the scriptures with the sacrament. Its very position in the rite, scripture-homily-sacrament, shows its integrating function: what Jesus announces in his Word he will fulfill in the sacrament, and the homily should make this intrinsic connection clear.

Every parable and miracle story is a promise of the Spirit. Thus the miracle that Jesus performs in the Gospel of the day occurs today when in the Eucharist the Christian touches Jesus with faith, as did the woman with the issue of blood (Mark 5:29), or is touched by him, as happened to the daughter of Jairus (Mark 5:40). This is not a call merely to remember the past; this is not a quaint way of speaking allegorically but a sacramental reality. The miracle is happening now. Both the apparition in the Upper Room recounted in John 21 and the apparition to the disciples of Emmaus in Luke 24 are told by the evangelists with such obvious eucharistic allusions that the appearance of the Risen Jesus is presented as a reality that occurs each time the Eucharist is celebrated. The past comes into the present.

This is exactly what Jesus did in the synagogue of Nazareth (Luke 4). His homily on the Isaian text was brief and poignant: "Today has this scripture been fulfilled in your midst" (Luke 4:21). He brings the past into the present by affirming that God's will to save is present and active here and now. His hearers were filled with awe and delight (Luke 4:22). That same awe and delight is given to the congregation when the homilist is able to capture the "today" dimension of the scripture of the day.

In contrast with other forms of preaching, like pre-evangelization, evangelization, and catechesi, the homily to which the dogmatic constitution *Verbum Dei* (24) gives "pride of place," is kerygmatic—it proclaims an event. It does not elaborate an intellectual doctrinal argument. It speaks to the heart rather than to the head. It makes the link between the Word "then" as contained in scripture and the lives of the congregation hearing that Word "now." It is meant to be "spirit and life," and is linked to the liturgical readings, unlike the other forms of preaching. The term *homily,* whose etymological root implies familiar conversation, was used by the *Constitution on the Liturgy* to distinguish it from the three other forms of "sermons" which are not kerygmatic and which, although they use scriptural texts, do not necessarily use those of the eucharistic liturgy of the day.

Since Vatican II, homilies have become more biblical. That is already an accomplishment compared to the catechetical and moralistic sermons of an earlier epoch. The problem now is that many priests have not grasped the interpretive role of scripture in their homilies, how the Word of God the people just heard must touch their lives. The pastoral document on homiletics issued by the United States Bishops' Committee on Priestly Life and Ministry, *Fulfilled in Your Hearing* (USCC 1982), went considerably beyond the *Constitution on the Liturgy* when it stated that the purpose of the homily was not merely to explain scripture but to use scripture to shed light on human existence (29, 20). *Fulfilled in Your Hearing* equivalently calls for what Andrew Greeley terms "correlative preaching," linking faith with life. The privileged moment to do this is the liturgy.

To correlate faith and life through the scriptures means the priest must grasp the literal meaning of the sacred text. For this he has at his disposal the tools of biblical criticism whose insights can be obtained from biblical commentaries and homiletic source material. Although he will not make this literal meaning the goal of the homily, the homilist must grasp it himself or he will lose his focus on the text. His homily will become a "sermon" detached from the text. It will become a free-floating kite without a string.

The homilist does not stop at the literal meaning; he must show the text's relevance for people today. In order to do this, he must be aware of where people are. He must take the issues Jesus addresses and apply them to people's needs. "The homilist should keep in mind the mystery that is being celebrated and the *needs of the particular community*" (emphasis added) (*General Instruction of the Roman Missal, 41*).

This is just another way of saying that the homilist must share Jesus' pity for the crowds, "anxious and helpless" (Matt 9:36). He must address the realities we tend to repress because they are too threatening: our guilt for the past, our lack of showing our love in the present, and our anxiety over our future death. The homilist must invite people to become present to themselves and to their needs. This is the task of spirituality. He must show how faith offers hope in the areas of deepest human concern. That was how Jesus preached the good news. For Zacchaeus it was being forgiven and having his guilt removed. For the Samaritan woman it was Jesus' offer of living water, the Spirit of love.

For the sister of Lazarus it was to hear the words: "Those who believe in me, even though they die, will live, and everyone who lives and believes in me will never die" (John 11:25–26).

Both the *Constitution on the Liturgy* and the *Sacramentary* assume the homilist must be a spiritual father to his congregation.

> By means of the homily…*the guiding principles of the Christian life* are expounded from the sacred text during the course of the liturgical year. (Constitution on the Liturgy, 52)

And again,

> The homily is strongly recommended as an integral part of the liturgy and as *a necessary source of nourishment of the Christian life.*…The homilist should keep in mind the *mystery that is being celebrated and the needs* of the particular community (emphasis added). (*General Instruction of the Roman Missal,* 41)

Being a spiritual father is a role that often embarrasses priests who have not had training in spiritual direction or who have not experienced being directed. But the principles of gospel spirituality presented are fundamentally simple. A presbyter who knows these principles and their dynamic and who lives this spirituality will have confidence in his role as spiritual father to his congregation. He will offer life and hope to people, especially those who are leading lives of not-so-quiet desperation.

This is the essential message of Jesus' preaching in the Eucharist: "My blood of the New Covenant shed for you.…" God wants the homilist to show how he is dealing with us and trying to get through to us despite our resistance. He wants him to preach with conviction that a bold love-will is at work in history. The presbyter must preach the central role God intends the Eucharist to play in the spiritual life.

In the scripture readings on which the homilist will be preaching, he will see God calling his people to share his *dream* of what our daily life could be. He will encounter a Jesus who experiences moments of deep *dissatisfaction* with the competitiveness and lack of faith he finds among his followers. Many times in the prophetic books, the homilist will find God frustrated at Israel's waywardness.

This contrast between what we could be and what we are reveals the desire in God's heart, the *desire* he wants us to share with him. Filled with the desire to get to where we could be, we tend to make a massive effort, but it's nothing but a *detour,* a very human way of acting. Eventually it leads to *despair.* We will never be able to scale the mountain. Only now will we hear the invitation of Jesus: "Ask" (Matt 7:7). We are invited to send out distress signals, asking God for what we need to fulfill his dream. "Set me on a cliff too high for me to reach" (Ps 27:5).

God wants a homilist who has himself experienced and grasped this pattern with its promise: "the one who humbles him/herself will be exalted" (Luke 18:14). Unless he experiences this pattern himself, he will not preach with conviction. The presbyter who experiences this spirituality in his own life is ready to preach effectively.

The ministry of the presbyter involves total dedication; it is not a job he can detach himself from. His very preaching ministry "drags" him into holiness. His spirituality will be dialectical: he prays in order to preach but he preaches in order to pray, as Donald Cozzens has pointed out.[2] As he prepares his homily he must read the scripture of the day, hear the promises that passage contains, and reflect on where both he and his congregation are and finally how this scripture offers hope and healing. In preparing the homily, the priest will get insights into human nature and the divine purpose. In the banality of preparing the homily, he will see how the mystery of grace unfolds in history and in people's lives. The preparation of the homily can become an event in which he experiences the divine consciousness being shared with him and through him with the congregation. As he hears himself preaching God's will and love, the homilist hears himself called to the same conversion he calls his hearers to. He must get drunk on the same wine he offers to the congregation, said Humbert of Romans, an early Master General of the Dominican Order.[3] Donald Cozzens goes so far as to say that

> the encouragement to preach a homily at daily celebrations of Eucharist as well as Sunday celebrations is the major structural development in the spirituality of the priest emanating from the Second Vatican Council. For the daily homily demands prayer and reflections, study and contemplation. It calls for the priest to acquire the imagination of the novelist and the heart of the poet.[4]

Having become present to himself through gospel spirituality, one of the homilist's principal responsibilities is to make the congregation present to itself. Just as he experiences this in his own life, his hearers will seek redemption only if they are aware of their needs. What links preaching to life, what transforms prayer from cliché to energizing encounter with God, is getting in touch with one's inner pain. The process by which God comes to us and deals with us arises out of our need, and the homilist must be attuned to this fact as the *Sacramentary* points out (*General Instruction of the Roman Missal,* 41). The homily becomes a means of helping people discover their wounds. We shy away from moving into this area of pastoral ministry because it is not easy to look at our wounds, especially if we have little hope for a cure. The homilist will lead people into their repressed fears only when he knows from experience that exaltation comes out of it. It is fruitless to try to teach someone how to swim if you yourself have never learned how to float by trusting the water.

Making the hearers present to themselves is what we mean by prophetic preaching. *We can be redeemed only to the extent to which we see ourselves.*[5] For Paul it is prophecy that is the greatest charism, not speaking in tongues (1 Cor 14:24–25). The prophet admonishes the hearer and elicits a confession of guilt that anticipates the last judgment. He sheds light on the dark areas of a person's life. Then that person's eyes are opened, as happened to David when he was admonished by Nathan's prophetic preaching (2 Sam 12).

Without prophetic preaching, we end up with a form of preaching that affirms the congregation without challenging it to new growth in the areas of faith and love. We preach the kind of statements we often see on banners in our churches, giving people false assurances that they are doing OK. When our basic message is "I'm OK, you're OK," we ignore the fact of our divided hearts and reinforce people in their lack of faith. We fail to challenge them to grow in faith.

Jesus made the apostles into great preachers. How did he form them? He did not give them false assurances that they were doing fine. On the contrary, he took them down the path of honesty: "You have little faith" (Matt 8:26; 14:31); "You are slow to believe" (Luke 24:25); "Why are you fearful?" (John 6:20); "How long must I put up with you?" (Mark 9:19); "Are you totally without understanding?" (Mark

8:17, 21); "When the Son of Man comes do you think he will find faith on the earth?" (Luke 18:8) "Nowhere in all of Israel have I seen such faith [as in this pagan]" (Matt 8:10).

Jesus did not succeed in bringing the apostles to a faith that did not depend on signs until they became convinced that they had no faith, and that they were infected with the yeast of sign-faith. Calvary convinced them that they had no faith, that they didn't believe Jesus' promise that God was bringing in the kingdom through his death. There was a chilling moment when Jesus appeared to them on Easter Sunday night. What shame, what embarrassment in meeting the friend they had abandoned in his hour of greatest need. They eventually saw that they were filled with repression in spite of spending three years with him. After the resurrection they were incredibly humble. The church was born out of the apostles' experience of the forgiveness they received from the Risen Jesus.

If a presbyter is not in touch with his own divided heart—if he is not conscious of his own lack of faith—he will never preach prophetically, but will reaffirm people in their lack of faith. It is interesting that after Jesus "upbraided [the apostles] for their lack of faith" (Mark 16:14), he immediately tells them, "Go and preach the gospel to the whole world" (Mark 16:15). They were ready to preach once they knew how little faith they had.

The apostles entered into the process of preaching that Jesus marked out for them, preaching from their weakness. They preached the splendor of Jesus and at the same time their shabby response. Their deep humility enabled their hearers to enter into their own sinfulness. In their preaching the apostles confessed their sins: their flight from Calvary, their denials, their refusal to hear what Jesus told them, their competitiveness, their lack of faith. All this is recorded in the Gospels, which are in large part a confession of the apostles' sins. They effectively said to their hearers: "You think you did poorly! Listen to us!" Such humility invited their hearers to admit their guilt: "Yes, we keep missing the point too." Thus their humble leadership into the truth set their hearers free to enter into their weakness. If the homilist's prayer life has made him aware of his sinfulness and lack of faith, he will preach effectively because he will preach with humility.

The Emmaus incident (Luke 24) is a marvelous model of prophetic and correlative preaching. Jesus *engaged* the two disciples, not by giving them answers to questions they were not asking, but by starting where they were, in deep depression over their disappointed hope concerning him: "We had been hoping...." He got them to talk about what they were feeling.

Then Jesus used the Hebrew scriptural tradition to shed light on their problem. He *informed* them. In so many words he said: "You need not have been disappointed in Jesus of Nazareth. Scripture shows that the cross was firmly planted in the heart of Israel: Abraham and Isaac's sacrifice, the suffering of the Hebrew children at the time of the Passover and the Exile, the Suffering Servant, Daniel, Susanna, and so many others. The Christ of God, not the Christ of human making, *had* to suffer" (Luke 24:26). He *had* to enter the human condition and take it to himself or he would have been irrelevant to us. The real pain of suffering is in its isolating aspect, but the suffering Messiah assures us that he has experienced our human tragedy. We are not alone or isolated, for our God has gone there before us—he "is near to the brokenhearted" (Ps 34:18). "Because he himself was tested by what he suffered, he is able to help those who are being tested" (Heb 2:18).

At a certain moment they are *transformed* as they hear him reveal the discrepancy between their false convictions and the biblical tradition. They experience a moment of terrible insight. They see that they have been refusing to listen to him on the road to Jerusalem as he told them the Messiah had to be the Suffering Servant. They see that they had been in deep denial. They must have said to themselves, "How could we have missed it? He was telling us this all along and we turned a deaf ear. We made a god and messiah in our own image, but God had something much better for us." Their transformation gave them an insight that pierced their hearts. Now they accepted their guilt and desired forgiveness. When they arrived at Emmaus they would not let go of Jesus, who had unraveled for them the mystery of a suffering messiah: "Stay with us; the day is almost over and it is getting dark" (Luke 24:29).

What Jesus had done was to get them into their need. He *engaged* them. Then he *informed* them. Finally, he brought them to a moment of insight that *transformed* them. The homilist must work this transformation in the congregation with his homily.

If priests bring faith and love to their ministry of preaching, if they preach prophetically, if they share Jesus' pity for the crowds, that ministry will sanctify them and fill them with joy. It is the joy of offering gospel hope and not a hope that springs from superficial props. This is the joy that produces good homilies and happy priests. When they shed light on human existence, especially on the problem of evil, their people will not let go of them as the disciples of Emmaus would not let go of Jesus. The homily must supply the eucharistic assembly with the reason why they should "lift up their hearts" and "give thanks to the Lord our God," even in the midst of encircling gloom. Unless the homilist has told them why, he has no right to say those words.

Andrew Greeley and Donald Cozzens put great emphasis on the priest's use of the imagination. Jesus' preaching involved a move into the world of the imagination, where the battle for the human heart is either won or lost. The divine will doesn't operate through a divine imagination, nor do the angels have angelic imaginations—once they know the good their will immediately goes out to it. But human wills do not move without attractive images. God who made human nature knows this and is therefore in the image-making business: the *Logos* in his human nature and the sacraments of the church are images that invite the surrender of the human heart. Without images preaching is abstract. It becomes cold creedal statements. This was not Jesus' way: "I preach only in parables" (Matt 13:34; Mark 4:33). If only the homilist knew the power of the image in selling his product as Madison Avenue does in selling soap and cereal.

The scriptural incident in the Gospel of the day is often so well known it has no effect. It has become trite. The homilist must use his imagination to get a good story that illustrates what the Gospel said. If he finds the right story, one that fits what Jesus is doing or saying, and develops it in the homily, all he has to do at the end is say: "Isn't that what the Gospel today was all about?" This avoids the lethal effect on the congregation produced by retelling the Gospel passage in one's own words. To find the right example or story is key, not a story that is told for its own sake but in function with the Gospel narrative. One image is worth a thousand words. The homilist himself may not have a reservoir of stories from his own experience, but he can draw on the experiences of others supplied by literature, good theater, and films.

Part of the asceticism of being an effective homilist is searching for new and relevant images. To choose to become a preacher and homilist is to choose to move into the world of the imagination, like Jesus. To bypass the imagination, is to bypass the human heart.

Of course, for the priest to preach well he must appreciate the centrality of the Eucharist for the spiritual life. He must grasp that essential message Jesus has embodied in his Eucharist. He must know the gospel path by which God works and gets through to us; he must test that path by living it. Then there is the craft. The homilist must learn to preach in images. The imagination must get in touch with the full reality of our humanity, with its horrors *and* joys. This in turn produces a realism that is essential to the priest's pursuit of holiness.

Anyone, priest or layperson, who has grasped the dynamics of gospel spirituality will find an echo and a reinforcement of that spirituality in almost every liturgical and scriptural text used in the liturgy. It is a joy to discover these principles of gospel spirituality embedded in the texts of the Mass. As we come to recognize these principles and begin putting them into practice in our lives, the integration of personal piety with objective liturgy will begin.

We have devoted much time to the presbyter as the one who presides over the liturgy of the Word. The informed Catholic layperson can tap into the riches the liturgy contains even in defective liturgies. There is no value in abdicating responsibility for our spiritual life by faulting poor presiders or homilists.

What can the layperson seeking the integration of personal piety with the church's liturgy do? How best can we prepare for liturgy? The liturgy itself gives a hint: *My brothers and sisters, to prepare ourselves to celebrate the sacred mysteries let us call to mind our sins* (Penitential Rite, Introduction C). The very condition for entering into the liturgy is the journey inward, the asceticism of becoming present to oneself, the willingness to humble oneself by looking at the dark side of our divided hearts. The liturgy itself presumes there is spirituality at work going on outside the liturgy because the liturgy itself does not leave time for much introspection. The discovery of sins and sinfulness occurs through the monitoring of our choices, and that goes on outside the liturgy. The penitential rite presupposes the ability to experience our sinfulness readily.

The best preparation for liturgy consists in *becoming real,* so that our real life will prepare us for the Eucharist. The liturgy is a descending gift of the Spirit. We can't produce that. The liturgy presupposes the asceticism of cultivating receptivity for the descending Gift. We will only be receptive to the degree we see our need for the Spirit. The coming of faith and love into our life through the Eucharist is the kingdom. It is the beginning of the eschatological banquet Jesus pointed to and wants us to be preoccupied with.

We should be surprised like those who encounter royal messengers inviting them to the palace. But so often we do not feel the slightest surprise at being invited to the Eucharist. It doesn't seem to be an appropriate reaction. What if we received an invitation to have lunch with just the president Tuesday next? We might call up the White House to see if there's been some mistake.

To enter the Eucharist we must be willing to be open to our actual human feelings: hatred, contempt, self-righteousness, self-justification, judgments. If we don't come to the liturgy conscious of our divided hearts and those areas of our lives that are yet unredeemed, the liturgy of redemption passes us by. The best preparation for liturgy is to present ourselves to God exactly where we are.

The pagan Celsus was the spokesman for much of paganism when he attacked the gospel of forgiveness as cheap grace:

> Those who summon people to the other mysteries make this preliminary proclamation: "Who has pure hands and a wise tongue...[come forward]...." But let us hear what these Christians call: "Whoever is a sinner, whoever is unwise, whoever is a child, and, in a word, whoever is a wretch, the Kingdom of God will receive him."[6]

Celsus grasped that the eucharistic liturgy has a direct relation to sinners, not the righteous. He surmised that it is crucial to enter the Christian mysteries with one's wounds. Preparation of the Mass texts beforehand will help, but the best preparation is to come with our sinfulness. Here we can meet the real God. Here we can be strengthened, healed, and invited into intimacy. All else is illusion. For those living in illusion God can do nothing, for only the real world is God's. If we dare to come out of our illusions into the real world, God can take care of every need we have. The goal of spirituality is precisely to call us out of illusion.

Just as the priest will not be an effective homilist unless he sees the centrality of the Eucharist and how Jesus preaches his essential message through it, so laypeople cannot enter into the liturgy unless they see the Eucharist as central to the Christian life for which their spiritual life is the preparation.

When we come down to it, the liturgical reform of the past four decades gave us a set of new liturgical books. Our work now is in the area of preaching and catechesis, opening up the riches of gospel spirituality the new books contain. Until we have tapped into the spirituality and ecclesiology of those new books, we will give the impression that the reform was about replacing old rubrics with new rubrics, much ado about nothing. Some critics feel that we have a lifeless reform without any genuine renewal. The objective of this book is to show that what appears to some to be a lifeless reform can become a dynamic renewal by bringing the spirituality of the individual into an integrated harmony with the public prayer of the church.

Until homilists are in touch with the real nature of the reform and the spirituality, ecclesiology, and sacramental theology behind it, they will not be of much help to Catholics who are often well versed in theology and liturgy and are looking for direction on how to make their spiritual lives one with the liturgy of the church and how to make the liturgy their own prayer. This book was meant to help supply that direction both for presider-homilists and for the people in the pews.

Notes

Chapter One

1. Bede K. Lackner, S.O.Cist., *The Eleventh Century Background of Citeaux*, Cistercian Publications (Washington, D.C.: Consortium Press, 1972), p. 169.

2. Irenée Hausherr, *Spiritual Direction in the Early Christian East*, trans. Anthony P. Gythiel (Kalamazoo, Mich.: Cistercian Publications, 1990), p. 30.

3. Clifford Longley, "Treading the Mystical Pathway," *The Times* (London), March 12, 1984.

4. Louis Bouyer as quoted by Harvey Egan, S.J., *What Are They Saying About Mysticism?* (New York: Paulist, 1982), p. 2.

Chapter Two

1. Gerhard von Rad, *The Message of the Prophets*, trans. D. M. G. Stalker (London: SCM, 1968), p. 42.

2. Doris Lessing, *The Sirian Experiments* (New York: Alfred A. Knopf, 1981), p. 212.

3. Doris Lessing, *Shikasta* (New York: Alfred A. Knopf, 1979), p. 90.

4. As quoted in Steven Marcus, *Engels, Manchester, and the Working Class* (New York: W.W. Norton, 1985), pp. 182–183.

5. Kurt Vonnegut, *The Sirens of Titan* (New York: Dell, 1972), pp. 271–72.

6. Edwin Markham, *Outwitted*, in *The Shoes of Happiness and Other Poems* (Garden City, N.Y.: Doubleday, Page & Co., 1915), p. 1.

7. H. F. M. Prescott, *The Man on a Donkey* (New York: Charles Scribner's Sons, 1966), p. 585.

8. H. A. Reinhold as quoted by K. Pecklers, *The Unread Vision* (Collegeville, Minn.: Liturgical, 1998), p. 143.

Chapter Three

1. Marcus Barth, *Ephesians: Introduction, Translation, and Commentary (I–III)*, vol. 34 of *The Anchor Bible* (Garden City, N.Y.: Doubleday, 1974), p. 127.

Chapter Four

1. Joachim Jeremias, *New Testament Theology*, trans. John Bowden, vol. 1 (New York: Charles Scribner's Sons, 1971), p. 152.

2. *The Spiritual Exercises of St. Ignatius*, trans. Louis J. Puhl, S.J. (Chicago: Loyola University Press, 1951), p. 35, para. 74.

Chapter Five

1. *The Coptic Gospel of Thomas*, logion 28, in Herbert Musurillo, S.J., *The Fathers of the Primitive Church* (New York: New American Library, 1966), p. 121.

2. Prescott, *op. cit.*, p. 585.

3. Joachim Jeremias, *Rediscovering the Parables* (New York: Charles Scribner's Sons, 1966), p. 122.

4. Barth, *op. cit.,* pp. 65–127 *passim*.

5. Joseph Ratzinger, *Introduction to Christianity*, trans. J. R. Foster (New York: Herder and Herder, 1970), p. 192.

6. Adrienne von Speyr, *Confession,* trans. Douglas W. Stott (San Francisco: Ignatius, 1985), p. 21.

7. Ignatius of Antioch, *Letter to the Trallians*, VIII, 2.

8. Godfrey Diekmann, "The Reform of Catholic Liturgy," *Worship*, vol. 41, no. 3 (March, 1967), p. 150 f.

9. Jeremias, *New Testament Theology*, *op. cit.*, p. 116.

10. Albert Camus, *The Stranger*, trans. Stuart Gilbert (New York: Vintage Books, 1946), pp. 152–53.

11. Prescott, *op. cit.*, p. 585.

Chapter Six

1. Thomas F. Torrance, *The Doctrine of Grace in the Apostolic Fathers* (Grand Rapids, Mich.: Eerdmans, 1959).

2. *Ibid.*, p. v.

3. *Ibid.*, p. 136, footnote 2.

4. Emetrio de Cea, O.P., *Compendium of Spirituality* (New York: Alba House, 1996), p. 7.

5. Quoted by Frederic and Mary Ann Brussat, *Spiritual Literacy: Reading the Sacred in Everyday Life* (New York: Charles Scribner's Sons, 1996), p. 353.

6. Augustine, *Enchiridion* 117.

7. Karl Rahner, *Theological Investigations*, vol. I, trans. Cornelius Ernst, O.P. (New York: Crossroad, 1982), p. 310.

8. Joseph A. Fitzmyer, *The Gospel According to Luke: Introduction, Translation and Notes (X–XXIV)*, vol. 28 A of *The Anchor Bible* (Garden City, N.Y.: Doubleday, 1985), p. 1143.

9. St. Thomas Aquinas, *Summa Theologica*, II–II. Q. 83, art. 14.

10. Hans Urs von Balthasar, *Love Alone*, trans. Alexander Dru (New York: Herder and Herder, 1969), p. 51.

11. *Service Book and Hymnal of the Lutheran Church in America* (Minneapolis, Minn.: Augsburg, 1958), Collects and Prayers no. 96, p. 231.

12. Julian of Norwich, *Showings*, trans. Edmund Colledge, O.S.A., and James Walsh, S.J. (New York: Paulist, 1978), pp. 248 and 254.

13. F. X. Durrwell, C.SS.R., *In the Redeeming Christ*, trans. Rosemary Sheed (New York: Sheed and Ward, 1963), p. 143.

14. St. Francis de Sales, *Entretien Spirituel 2*, Oeuvres Complètes, vol. 3 (Paris: Louis Vivès, 1866), p. 282.

15. Quoted in Jules Lebreton, *The Spiritual Teaching of the New Testament*, trans. James E. Whelan (Westminster, Md.: Newman, 1960), p. 227, footnote 11.

16. Conrad Pepler, O.P., *The Three Degrees* (New York: Herder and Herder, 1957), p. 171.

17. *Dictionnaire de Spiritualité:* "Enfance Spirituelle," tome IV (Paris: Beauchesne, 1960), p. 691.

18. Simon Tugwell, *Prayer in Practice* (Springfield, Ill.: Templegate, 1974), p. 3.

19. St. Ambrose, *Exposition of Psalm 118*, nn. 12, 13–14 (*CSEL* 62, pp. 258–259).

20. *Letters of St. Ignatius of Loyola*, selected and translated by William J. Young (Chicago: Loyola University Press, 1959), p. 240.

21. Ruth Burrows, *Guidelines for Mystical Prayer* (London: Sheed and Ward, 1976), p. 132.

22. *Collected Letters of St. Thérèse of Lisieux*, ed. Abbé Combes, trans. F. J. Sheed (New York: Sheed and Ward, 1941), p. 289.

Chapter Seven

1. S. H. Cross and O. P. Sherbowitz-Weltzor, *The Russian Primary Chronicle* (Cambridge, Mass.: The Medieval Academy of America, 1953), p. 111.

2. Joseph Frank, *Dostoevsky: The Years of Ordeal* (Princeton: Princeton University Press, 1983), pp. 122–124.

3. Quoted in Jaroslav Pelikan, *The Emergence of the Catholic Tradition 100–600* (Chicago: University of Chicago Press, 1971), p. 29.

4. Franz Kafka, *Parables and Paradoxes* (New York: Schocken, 1961), p. 393.

5. Barth, *op. cit.*, p. 65.

Chapter Eight

1. Ignatius of Antioch, *Letter to the Romans*, VII, 3.

2. Joseph Ratzinger, *Being Christian*, trans. David Walls (Chicago: Franciscan Herald, 1970), p. 19.

3. Ignatius of Antioch, *Letter to the Smyrneans*, VI, 2.

4. Ceslaus Spicq, O.P., *Agape in the Synoptic Gospels*, trans. Sr. Mary Aquinas McNamara, O.P., and Sr. Mary Honoria Richter, O.P. (St. Louis: B. Herder, 1963), pp. 79–80.

Chapter Nine

1. Justin Martyr, *First Apology*, chapter 67.

2. Donald B. Cozzens, "The Spirituality of the Diocesan Priest" in *Being a Priest Today*, ed. Donald J. Goergen, O.P. (Collegeville, Minn.: Liturgical, 1992), p. 63.

3. Simon Tugwell, O.P., *Ways of Imperfection* (Springfield, Ill.: Templegate, 1985), p. 138 f.

4. Cozzens, *op. cit.*, p. 70.

    5. Quoted in George F. Simons, *Keeping Your Personal Journal* (New York: Paulist, 1978), p. 30.

    6. Pelikan, *op. cit.,* p. 29.